SUNRISE AT MIDNIGHT

My Journey From Head to Heart

By

Nancy Stutz-Martin

DEDICATION

My husband, Tony Martin, whose love and sacrifice made this project a reality; to my son, Pastor John Stutz, whose encouragement, prayers, and unwavering belief in me has been endless; to very special friends who have lifted up endless prayers, provided support for me, and believed in me when I couldn't; to my dearest friend and fellow laborer for the cause of healing God's children, Reverend Edward Langham, Jr.; to my dear cousin, Ruth Taylor; to my faithful friend, Carol Elmore Standifer; to Margaret Baker, Carol Rimasfski, and the rest of my church family at Chickamauga Presbyterian; to the Board of Directors at Sunrise At Midnight.

I would also like to thank Bishop Joey Johnson for his encouragement and for sharing his Biblical knowledge and wisdom with me over the years. I want to acknowledge Pastor Glenn Murphy for his amazing heart, for being sensitive to the Holy Spirit, and being the catalyst for the healing in his church staff as well as in his community.

I'm also thankful to Russell and John at The Grief Recovery Institute for opening their hearts and their lives to me. They shared their love and vision, and in so doing, taught me skills to help others to then reach more people who learned to be free. We often laugh and call Grief Recovery® the "Get Out of Jail Card." And isn't that what Jesus commanded us to do—to set the captives free?

And finally, I want to thank all the incredible, courageous grievers whom I've worked with over the past twelve years who gave me my research and blessed my life beyond words.

TABLE OF CONTENTS

Forward
Introduction
Overview
Lessons From My Journey of Healing

This book was edited and reformatted for publishing from Nancy Stutz-Martin's doctoral dissertation. The jacket design was created by Mike Wadel from the SUNRISE AT MIDNIGHT logo.

FORWARD

In 1990 I was diagnosed with a life-threatening condition called systemic sclerosis, which causes arteries to harden and prevents blood flow to vital organs, such as the lungs, kidneys, and heart. At the rate my condition was progressing, my doctor estimated that, at best, I had only a few years to live. I could have received disability benefits and quit my job as a medical technologist, but I was a single mother, and the thought that my fourteen-year-old son might be taken from me by his father or by foster care was more than I could bear. So I continued working.

The disease soon began to ravage my body. I became so fatigued that I could barely stand up at work and after a couple of hours, I was holding onto the counter to keep from falling. I was in constant, agonizing pain and had to take massive doses of Procardia just to keep my arteries open.

I'd seen so many patients roll over and give up when they were given a negative diagnosis, but because of my belief in God, I understood that there was a great power within me. My highest goal was to enjoy the time I had left. If I only had five days, I wanted them to be five good days. I allowed myself to pray for one thing: to see my son graduate from high school. If God, in His mercy, could extend my life that long, then my son would be an adult, and I would have been able to prepare him to face life's responsibilities on his own. I knew in my heart that in God's infinite wisdom He knew what was best for me, so I never asked Him to heal me.

In the meantime, I embraced each day as a gift, reading medical books about my condition and vowing not to give up. None of my doctors could understand how someone with so much debilitating arterial damage could continue to pursue life and handle all the daily responsibilities of ordinary living. They'd study my medical reports and then look at me, and shake their heads. The woman with such an active life didn't equate with the seriously sick woman on their charts.

Early on, I had made two lists of all the things I wanted to do before I died. The first list contained all the necessary things, like a living will and medical power of attorney. The second listed all the things I just felt like doing, and on the top of that list was: Go back to school!

During my son's high school graduation ceremony, tears slipped down my face. My merciful God had indeed given me the desire of my heart. And three months later, I drove my son to Tennessee Technical College, helped him unload his stuff at his dorm, and continued on to Nashville, where I'd begin a master's program for Psychiatric Nurse Practitioners at Vanderbilt University.

Since I had a pre-existing condition, I wouldn't be eligible for the same health insurance if I changed jobs, so on weekends; I commuted two hours to Chattanooga to work my lab job at Memorial Hospital. Driving back and forth provided an undisturbed opportunity for me to talk with God, and I took advantage of that quiet time. Our relationship deepened during those years.

One of the ways I'd sought relief during my illness was to sit in my hammock. It was the kind without wooden bars on each end, so when you sit in it, the rope sides wrap completely around you as you're suspended in air. I visualized God's loving arms holding me in space, and with my feet off the ground, I was in His complete control.

During those times of resting in God's arms, He'd shown me a ministry to help others who were dealing with life-threatening illnesses. I knew my calling was to empower people to deal with their grief and loss and move on to find beauty in life again. The more I thought about it, the more I realized how strange it was that someone like me could work in hospitals for over twenty years and never learn how to help people respond in a positive way to the inevitable changes of life. Most of those changes incorporated loss in some form:

- loss of a relationship because of a change such as graduation, promotion, moving, or
- loss of the presence of someone due to death or divorce,
- loss of a hope, a dream, or an expectation.

Graduate schools, medical schools, and seminaries train students from an intellectual standpoint, but loss is processed in the heart. An intellectual approach can provide knowledge and understanding, but it doesn't bring recovery. Intellectual knowledge only teaches us to "cope." I believe there's more to life than "coping." God calls us to be joyful and at peace. Yet, I couldn't find the tools to achieve joy and peace in the face of loss. No one teaches us how to respond effectively to loss. We sit with our arms folded in pain, while God is urging us to open our arms and receive His abundant grace.

In graduate school I kept telling my professors that they weren't giving me everything I needed to help my clients. I knew there was a "missing piece," yet I had no clue as to what it was. So I trusted God to lead me on a journey to find it.

While attending a class at Sloan Kettering Cancer Institute in New York City, I discussed this idea with a fellow student. He told me that he'd found the "missing piece" in California, at The Grief Recovery Institute in Los Angeles. He explained how the concepts of Grief Recovery® had helped hundreds of thousands of people deal successfully with loss. I was excited, and felt in my heart that God wanted me to go.

I completed the Grief Recovery® Certification class and was impressed with the practical steps for dealing with a complicated, emotional process. It so transformed my life and the quality of work I was able to do with clients that I decided to counsel people exclusively in grief recovery.

Over the past twelve years, I've worked extensively with the church, at the individual, congregational, and leadership level, both in the United States and abroad. I've witnessed the sad fact that most people lack the basic skills to deal with their losses. I've also observed that Grief Recovery® tools truly work, regardless of the type of loss, and that the process transcends cultures.

I love my work, but because writing is not a priority, the Lord patiently, but persistently, made it clear to me that I needed to sit down and complete this book. There are a plethora of wonderful Christian books that remind us of our position in Christ. There are volumes about freedom and joy, and books about significant challenges facing the church. Too often we read these books, become excited, feel a spiritual awakening, and then a few days later, our zeal wears off, and we return to our old way of living.

Have you ever wondered why our excitement wears off? I believe it's because most books simply engage our minds, and our hearts are unmoved. A transformed heart translates into changed behavior. God asked us to worship in spirit and in truth, aspects of a pure heart, and yet, for most of us, our minds are in much better shape than our hearts.

This book is about healing our hearts. It offers a practical and scriptural basis for its Grief Recovery® principles. It provides readers with the tools that can assist them to resolve their losses and grief and become mature followers of Christ.

Introduction

As a Board Certified Psychiatric Nurse Practitioner, I'm able to function in the capacity of a therapist and maintain a private practice. I also have prescriptive authority in the state of Tennessee, which means I may write prescriptions for my clients. In January 1996, I began incorporating the skills I learned from the Grief Recovery® Certification Training into my private practice.

What I immediately began to see was that my clients no longer needed medications. I now had skills that would help them process the emotions attached to any of the losses that had already occurred in their lives, as well as those that would inevitably come along in the future. These clients no longer needed to medicate their pain. This eliminated many inappropriate or destructive behaviors as well.

At least ninety percent of the time, the underlying issue that counselors see relates to unresolved loss. Because of this fact, I knew that with these tools, I was well on my way to making a big difference in the lives of my clients. But I had no idea how big!

I began working with Hospice patients and their families, and the results so astounded me, that I began investing my professional and private time in sharing and teaching these skills as a Grief Recovery® Specialist. Here's the story of the first family I counseled with Grief Recovery® techniques. I include it so the reader will more fully appreciate why I'm so devoted to this work, and also because it's an example of the thousands of individuals I've worked with who have deeply benefited from Grief Recovery®. Bob and Mary had twin sons who had contracted AIDS. They were in their late twenties.

Bob and Mary belonged to a Baptist church. When they shared that their sons needed prayer because they were dying from AIDS, all the couple received were cold, judgmental comments. No one seemed to care about Mary and Bob's feelings; instead, they insinuated that there must have been something wrong with their parenting that these sons had turned out gay. This is the testimony of Bob and Mary:

In March 1995, our son Steve died, and we were devastated. Steve was one of our twin sons, and, for years, he had seemed to be the "glue" which held our family together. Most days he phoned each of our four other children and us, carrying family news back and forth. Many days he called us several times, just to see how we were doing and to see if we needed his help with anything. He had a deep commitment to his family.

But we were unable to grieve for Steve in the normal way. You see, his twin brother was also terminally ill. We just couldn't take the chance that our open grief would damage Bobby's immune system any faster than was already happening. So we had only brief moments in the back bedroom or hall to hold each other and cry silently.

In many ways, Bobby was sicker than Steve. Even before Steve died, I had to half-carry Bobby into the clinic, asking for help. While Bobby was being given medical attention, I was called aside and told the best thing I could do for him was to take him home and give him plenty of tender loving care. I couldn't accept that, and we continued to do everything humanly possible to help Bobby live.

But fifteen months after losing Steve, Bobby died, too. My wife and I went into a freefall. The grief and depression were so black and deep, we felt we would never see the light of day again. Interest in life and everything about it was gone. For six months we were immobilized, she on one bed, and I on another.

It was a wonder that we saw the notice in the paper for the Grief Recovery® class that Nancy facilitates. Nancy had come by our home a few times just after Bobby's death, and we knew what a wonderful, caring person she was. So we enrolled in her course immediately.

It was one of the hardest things I have ever done. But it was also one of the most rewarding. Clearly, Nancy saved our lives. This course forces you to face the darkest moments of your life and gives you the tools and practical skills to deal with them. At the seventh weekly meeting, I felt a thousand-pound weight lifting from my chest. The next morning I noted on my calendar: "Today, I started living again."

I still miss Bobby and Steve, but I know now that I have put the pieces of my life back together, and I can remember our good times while I move on.

For several years I continued leading Grief Recovery® groups. Then God dropped in my heart a burden for pastors and church leaders. I knew from the beginning that this process could be a key to revolutionizing "the church." Russell Frieberg, from Heritage Funeral Home, gave me my first opportunity to do a Grief Recovery® workshop for pastors. They sent out one hundred and twenty-five invitations to local pastors. Mr. Friedman confided in me that he anticipated that probably twelve to fifteen would show up. But Mr. Friedman didn't know that God had arranged this day. There were fifty people in attendance. Forty-five were pastors. I used that first experience to pour into them Grief Recovery® knowledge and the vision that God had dropped into my heart about healing His children.

The next morning I received a call from one of the pastors. He called to thank me and made the statement, "You will never know what healing went on in that room yesterday." After the shock settled, I realized that God had just sent His confirmation call. It was time to embark as a missionary to heal the body of Christ, but especially to reach church leadership, so healing could be facilitated at a global level.

Overview

I've been entrusted with a ministry of opening the eyes of my fellow pilgrims, and all those whose hearts are closed off to the voice of God because of all the hurts, pains, and injustices that they've encountered in a lifetime. Life on planet earth brings with it tears, agony, injustices, unanswered questions, and adversity. Such unresolved losses have given Satan a powerful stronghold on our churches today.

This unresolved pain crosses all cultural, ethnic, and denominational affiliations, preventing us from operating in the power that God ordained for us. Tragically, it prevents us from being a true comfort station for the world and creates a stumbling block in our ability to reach the lost and un-churched.

We come into this world as loving, trusting, open, and honest individuals. When we experience our first event of broken trust, we start the process of building a wall around our heart, and internal messages of doubt and low self-worth begin to build. These messages drive our behaviors, no matter how much our minds try to stop them. We begin to take hold of habits and debilitating mindsets that set us up for a lifetime of reacting to life.

Over-achieving is an effort to bury the voices of self-doubt, but our accomplishments do nothing to resolve the emotional pain, nor do they stop the embedded messages in our heart and brain. So we continue striving, hoping that each new challenge will provide a different outcome. Instead, what we end up with, because life is difficult and full of afflictions, are more losses that remain unresolved.

I don't think there's a person alive who reaches adulthood without experiencing the grief that comes from a loss of trust. Loss-of-trust events include: broken promises, unanswered prayers, or betrayal. Maybe your mom never bought you the dress she promised, or maybe your dad died before you had a chance to reconcile. Maybe your daughter died after an operation when you trusted God to make her well. Maybe your wife left you for another man in the church, or maybe your boss didn't give you the promised raise or promotion. Maybe you suffered physical, sexual, or verbal abuse from a family member. Or you thought when you joined the church that Christians were different, only to have your expectations shattered.

Grief is about conflicting feelings. When a long illness ends in death, we might be relieved that the suffering is over, but then we can also experience fear, wondering how we'll enjoy life, pay our bills, or feel whole without that person. When an abusive relationship ends in divorce, we feel relief that the battle in our house is over, but we can also experience anger over what we perceive are "wasted years." Also, we might feel regret and fear, wondering if there will be another chance to find love in a new relationship. One could easily write a thousand-page book just listing loss-of-trust events and the conflicting mass of emotions that ensue, and still, the writer could not have expressed the deep way human beings endure pain.

One thing is certain, however. We can't replace the losses or change the disappointments in our lives. What we can do is change the way we relate to them, and that is what Grief Recovery ® actions are designed to help us to do.

Unless we examine our losses and work through these unresolved pain situations, destructive behaviors will be played out over and over again in our relationships, and the quality of our ministry or personal testimony will be affected. We create what's familiar to us, because if we're incomplete with the past, we inadvertently recreate it in the future.

So, Church, let's get to work! If unresolved pain and losses are holding so many of us down today, imagine a tomorrow where every one of us had a healed heart that guided our lives in service for the Lord! Imagine the power of His love pouring through your heart!

Even if you believe you've resolved the losses in your life, you need to understand the stranglehold these issues have on other people if you're to help them reach their full potential. How can they grasp how wide, long, and deep Christ's love is if they're holding onto past hurts and pains. How can they move victoriously in the future when they're unsuccessful in letting go of the painful past? How can they be filled to the measure of *all* the fullness of God? Somewhere deep inside, most of us know that God has called us to do more. Remember these verses from Ephesians:

I pray that out of His glorious riches, He may strengthen you with power through His Spirit in your *inner being*, so that Christ may dwell in your *hearts* through *faith*. And I pray that you, being rooted and established in love, may have power together with all the saints to grasp how wide and long and high and deep is the love of Christ, and to know this love that surpasses knowledge--that you may be filled to the measure of the *all fullness of God*. (Emphasis mine)[1]

No matter where we are on our spiritual journey, God is always calling us to a more intimate relationship with Him. To achieve this, we must take care of the unresolved grief first, by pouring out all the hurt and pain inside us, so that we can become an empty vessel to be filled up by God. Then, as we begin to establish Grief Recovery ® programs and ministries within the church and our communities, we will see the joy, power, and freedom that Jesus' sacrifice has provided.

Lessons from My Journey of Healing

Let us pray: "I pray that the eyes and ears of the enemy are closed to everything that takes place here today. Father, I pray that your host of heavenly angels would surround us, and that no eavesdroppers or unclean spirits of any kind could have any place in our midst today."

"I pray that our hearts, minds, souls, wills, and emotions would be turned to You in every way, and that the Holy Spirit would direct everything that takes place here, giving us supernatural ears to hear and eyes to see." (Then everyone said "Amen," sealing this protective decree.)

First I would like to thank my family, friends, and church family for all the love, support, and countless prayers that you have lifted up before the throne in my behalf. Words can't express how grateful I am.

It has not been an easy road. There were weeks that I never got out of bed, times when I could not lift my head off the pillow because I was so weak. I have always been extremely independent, but not this time. There were periods when Tony (my husband) and Jan (my nurse friend) had to take total care of me, bathing me, dressing me, putting my meds and food in my feeding tube. I went two months without consuming more than 500 calories a day, which affected by brain. They had to watch me like a hawk because I was not always rational. I was nauseated 24 hours a day for 4 months. For weeks everything I put in my body including water caused me to throw up. Imagine having a throat that is already solid blisters from the radiation and then when the acid from your stomach comes up in your throat how painful that is.

While it was not easy, It was comforting to know that you all were interceding for me. Thank you.

I was so excited to have the opportunity to share with you the things God has been teaching me throughout this journey. While collecting my thoughts for this testimony, it soon became apparent that there was no way I could share all the things in such a short period of time. So, I asked God to show me what was most important for you to hear today.

As I hit some of the highlights of my journey I invite you to listen for these key points:

1. Believe in miracles
2. Hearing the voice of God "My sheep hear My voice." How can we know God's specific will for us if we don't hear His voice? We have the written "Logos" word of God, the Bible, but it is general not always specific. Specifics that apply to us personally come from hearing the "Rhema" word of God, which is His voice.
3. Faith "Faith comes from hearing and hearing by the Word of God." Faith is an ACTION step on our part.
4. Treasures are found in dark places.
5. Suffering is not always bad, it can be redemptive.

Most of you know my story, but for those of you who don't:

I was working out at the gym five days a week and in the best health of my life. I was extremely excited about leaving on Sunday January 18[th]on my second trip to Africa. I couldn't wait to see the kids again and especially my little Aaron.

On the Tuesday before I was to leave I found myself in the recovery room hearing the doctor say, "you have stage 4 squamous cell carcinoma in the base of your tongue and 2, 3cm growths in your lymph glands."

I was stunned! How did I get from my exciting international mission work to here in the blink of an eye? I felt like I had been riding in a jet plane with God and someone opened the belly of the plane and "plop", I landed on the ground. It was a surreal experience that I just couldn't digest.

Now, I had to make a decision whether to leave on my 3 week trip to Africa or seek immediate medical attention as was suggested. My heart was broken over the thoughts of not seeing the children. I cried a lot at first, not over the cancer diagnosis but over not being able to go.

That night the Lord showed me a vision of a large wall. The wall looked familiar to me. Then the Lord said, "Nancy you have always figured out a way to go around the walls in your life or climb over them or move them out of the way. But not this time. This time you and I are going to walk straight through that wall together. You will keep your eyes focused on Me and we will walk straight through. This is not your time for Africa. This is your time with Me. This is for My glory.

Confirmation # 1 of my healing:

Fortunately I am blessed to have someone in my life who hears the voice of God and in whom I can trust to bring God's truth to a situation.

Within a few weeks, I received a call from this friend telling me she had been on her face for 2 days crying out to God for wisdom on how she could help me. The Lord gave her words for me which she faithfully wrote down. Incidentally, she is a Journaler - extraordinaire.

The day she brought God's words to me was a pivotal moment. It was then I knew and understood my assignment.

God's words are very personal and precious to me but I strongly believe I am to share excerpts with you. God's words are more powerful than any sermon.

"Nancy will be fine. She is undergoing all this trouble for My sake. It will not make sense now, but later she will hold this ordeal up to me as a living sacrifice. Her ills are not hers; they're Mine. They are a kind of sharing in My suffering.

No one asks why Yeshua had to be whipped and tormented that way, but that was part of His process. He was already Holy, but He needed greater understanding (in His human body) how I suffer.

Nancy's sufferings right now are not her own; they're Mine. I will see her though this. Tell her this is My way of seeing through her, letting My life pour through her entirely. I will fill her body completely with My Spirit. This is her gain, despite the suffering. Tell her to give all this pain to Me, so her suffering can be redemptive.

Most people do not understand redemptive suffering, but this ordeal is an answer to prayer. I will renew and cleanse her, heal her, lift her up she will be Mine and I will be hers. Yeshua understood this. His body was never his own, and yet He needed to understand My heart by being rejected and whipped and left alone up on that cross.

I want her to take this new step with Me, knowing it is for My good pleasure. We will endure the months ahead together, and she will gain, not lose. My glory will be all around her, and My favor will be obvious, despite the circumstances.

I will restore her to wholeness and she will know Me in a greater way, in a way she couldn't have imagined.

(People who are sold out to Me) will opt for certain things because they want more authority in Me. Every time someone overcomes the schemes of the enemy, their power and authority in Me increases. So the enemy loves to stir up trouble, but remember Job: I knew he could handle it (so I picked him). That is the picture. I don't put on anyone a test/trial that is too great. Because of Job's suffering, more will pass the test of (various losses) on earth, more whom the enemy might've destroyed will pass the test.

Remember always, laws are in place - when you pass a test in suffering, others by the law of continuance will pass the test."

(This is the way God explained it. The law of continuance is complex, but picture how when one man broke the 4-minute mile, then others around the world were suddenly able to. The same is true in every field: in science, a major discovery is made and suddenly, at around the same time, that same discovery is made around the world...one person's success alters the environment beyond our understanding and makes it possible for others. That is why God's elect suffer greatly---to help others succeed in their circumstances.)

"No trial is fun, but afterwards the fruit is great. Nancy's going through the circumstances she'll go through will help others she's never met or will meet. In this way her personal victory is greater than anything she can teach or say --- just by experiencing and turning to Me. (We succeed together.)

I will use every circumstance in her life to gain her a better understanding of Me and My Word, My Yeshua. True understanding comes from experience (revelation). I want her to go through what she'll go through in a way that will bring her closer to Me.

This is between Nancy and Me. It is for us to battle, to engage, to talk about, etc. It is a vehicle I am using to bring Nancy to another level. I didn't cause it; I'm using it...just as I have used other experiences in her life.

When people want to get closer to Me, I show them all My sides. I have shown Myself to Nancy as a healer - she has known Me in various ways. Now I want to be her companion through her suffering. I do not cause people to suffer illness; this fallen world causes that, but I bring redemption to suffering.

Nancy will pull through. She is battling, but I have ministering angels over her."

That was my 2nd confirmation of my healing. I knew beyond a shadow of a doubt because:
1. I believed in miracles.
2. I had heard the voice of God.
3. I chose to step out in faith and (take) Him at His word.

The Scripture says that God's words are irrevocable. If God said it then it is the truth. I chose to step out and stand on His word.

I also knew the power of words. I never said "I have cancer"; I said "I was diagnosed with cancer". I never took on the role of a "cancer patient"; I never said "I am a cancer patient". I knew I was healed from the beginning. But now after His words, my face was set like flint toward the goal and I refused to be moved despite what the doctors said.

In May Tony and I sat in the doctor's office listening to him say, "Nancy you are going to die, you have got to consume 2000 calories a day minimum to just survive the treatment." While in my head I am thinking you guys just don't get it. My Daddy said different and He has more power than you do. In a private conversation with Tony, the doctor said to him that he doubted my will to live. Tony assured the doctor that not only did I have the will to live but that God had promised me complete healing.

On my last radiation treatment the two women who unstrapped me from the table for the 35th time were crying. They said, "Nancy we are so happy! None of the staff believed that you would make it. This is a joyous day."

I had shared the words the Lord gave me with Tony and our son John. They believed at one level but as Tony watched me going downhill it was scary for him because he was afraid he was losing me. But they, just as my friends, only heard what "I" told them. They didn't hear God speak as I had.

I never asked to be healed. However God wanted it was OK with me. But by hearing His voice I knew what He wanted. In my spirit I knew, I never doubted.

After my first round of three high power chemo drugs I had a reaction to the 5FU, causing a week's stay in the hospital. Things were grim. I had no food for 13 days living on IV TPN. My potassium was down to 2!

I had an incredible experience at that lowest moment. I could literally feel the organs in my body shutting down. Then I heard this loud shout from my spirit, "No! God said she will not die so you must turn back on". And then I felt my organs beginning to slowly come back.

If I had not KNOWN God's will for me then I wouldn't be here today. Because the enemy wanted to take me out. It is no coincidence that the cancer was in my throat. Satan was trying to take out my voice so I couldn't continue sharing my faith.

But praise God I am here today, 100% cancer free doing exactly what Satan didn't want.

What can we learn from this experience?

1. Miracles are still happening 2000 years after Christ.
2. God is faithful when we step out. Remember the lady who had the issue of blood in Mark 5: 25-34? When she reached out and touched the hem of Christ's garment, He turned and said "woman your faith has healed you". If she had not stepped out and put her faith into action she would never have known her healing. God wants to give us a precious gift but he will not force it on us. He stands there with His arms reaching out but we have to do our part and step out to take it. Action on our part is the operative word.
3. Learning to hear God's voice can mean the difference between chaos, confusion, uncertainty and peace in the midst of the storm. A peace that brings steadfastness and the joy of the Lord.

Be clear that I did not say it prevents difficult times in our lives, because that is part of the Christian walk. But it does prevent UNNECESSARY pain, anxiety and fear.

Yes, you can have joy and peace in the midst of your darkest moment. I am a living example. That is God's promise to us: Isaiah 43:1-3 has been one of my favorite scriptures for years. God says in these verses "when we walk through the rivers we will not drown...when we walk through the fire we will not be burned...because I love you and you are precious to Me".

The peace and joy that comes is really hard to comprehend from a physical perspective. It is like being sheltered up under God's arms. It is so safe, secure and peaceful. As the chaos and uncertainty around you expands He just holds you closer and it doesn't matter. There is such a joy in knowing you are right where you are meant to be, sheltered in His arms.

Please understand that I am not implying in any way that it is wrong to be hurt and angry with God. It is very important to express your feelings to Him. He can handle them. What I am suggesting is don't stay there, get up and out and move forward, then the experience will not be as bad.

If we can learn to reframe our experience in those dark places it can change our experience. Reframe is a psychology term meaning to change the picture or change the way you perceive the picture.

Now God says the same thing in a different way in the Old Testament. In Isaiah 45; "our treasures are found in dark places". Much like what happens inside an oyster. The constant rubbing of the sand or irritant that enters the shell causes the oyster to produce a substance in an effort to protect its self. Over time in the dark waters the substance turns into a beautiful pearl.

So instead of looking at the picture about how bad it is, change it and search for the treasure for they are many. The precious time I have had with the Lord as a result of this experience, and the things He has taught me are more than worth everything I suffered. I can honestly say that if given an opportunity to go through this again I would be the first in the line, because the treasures far outweigh the pain and suffering!

Besides, it was an answer to my prayers. Some of you may remember me saying after my first trip to Africa, that I saw a level of believing and intimacy with God that I had never seen before and I wanted it. I thought I was a "pretty good Christian" until I got to Africa. I remember lying on a bench in the prayer garden in Mozambique looking up at the stars and crying out to God to be radically changed. I didn't want the status quo Christianity that I saw in the States. I wanted a deeper level of Him. I wanted more. God was so faithful. He answered my prayers. (Of course if He had asked me how He could answer that prayer I would have suggested a nice three-day spiritual retreat.)

When God is stirring things up in us it doesn't always feel good or comfortable. But just try to remember that is the time He is doing a Kingdom work in you and drawing you closer. And perhaps your experience will impact someone else that will change the Kingdom.

In closing I would like to share one story with you.

After church one Sunday in June 2009 a friend came up to me with big tears running down his face and said, "Nancy you are my miracle." I said what do you mean? Then we sat down and he began to share his story with me.

"For many years I was not totally committed to God. I was a believer but had become very attached to the things of this world. I knew God worked miracles but I wanted to see someone I knew healed. I told God if he would answer this prayer then I would give up and turn my whole life over to God. I was like doubting Thomas; I wanted to put my hand in the scar. That day in late May when you walked into our home I told my wife after you left that I knew God had healed you and that you were my miracle", he continued. "I have made a decision to let go of the world and give it all to God." It was at that moment God revealed this was one of the ways that completion of my assignment has impacted the Kingdom.

In second Corinthians 4:17 it says: "For our present troubles are small and won't last very long. Yet they produce for us a glory that vastly outweighs them and will last forever!

I never realized how true and powerful this verse was until I had this experience!

In His Grip,
Nancy
Dr. Nancy S. Martin

Chapter 1
GRIEF: 100% HEARTACHE

When human beings experience a loss, there's only one level of emotional intensity that comes next, one hundred percent undiluted heartache. Our losses are all painful to us. We don't have the ability to half hurt. We experience our pain at a hundred percent. Therefore, it's important to understand that we should never compare our losses. While it might seem from an intellectual perspective that the loss of a parent and the loss of a pet would have different emotional weight, in fact, that might not be true. What if that pet was the only living thing that gave you unconditional love? Your heart would still be broken at a hundred percent.

Grief is the normal and natural reaction to any significant emotional loss. We have been socialized to believe that life is about acquiring and holding onto things. Never once are we taught how to deal with the pain of losing something. It's no wonder we are not prepared to deal with one of life's most predictable experiences: loss.

Grief is not intellectual but rather a conflicting

mass of human emotions. It's our hearts that are broken not our heads. As long as we persist in intellectualizing grief, we'll continue to carry the pain. Comments such as, "You should be grateful you had him so long," or "At least she isn't suffering anymore" are meant to be helpful, and may even be true, but they don't help mend our broken hearts.

Grief will continue to affect our lives and those around us adversely when we're urged to accept the many myths about grief. Typical myths include such concepts as: bury your feelings, replace the loss, grieve alone, be strong for others, keep busy, and time heals all wounds. Recovery from loss does take some time, but it's the *actions* within that time frame that lead to successful recovery.

When a relationship ends, most of us automatically review the relationship and discover there are things we wish had been different. It's the incompleteness of the emotional relationship that results in our pain. Unresolved grief is almost always about undelivered communications of an emotional nature. There are a whole host of feelings that may be attached to those unsaid things. Happiness, sadness, love, fear, anger, relief, compassion, are just some of the feelings that a griever might experience. In your grief you do not need to categorize, analyze, or explain those feelings. You do need to learn how to communicate them and say goodbye to the relationship that has ended.[2]

Whether a loss is from the death of a loved one, a divorce, an ended relationship, a loss of trust, a loss of health, a loss of dreams, expectations, or hopes, the Grief Recovery® process can help you to move beyond your loss. In grief, you're not broken, and you don't need to be fixed. You don't need to be analyzed, criticized, or advised. You do, however, need to be listened to with dignity and respect.

Successful Grief Recovery® teaches a griever to have happy memories not turn painful, to retake a happy and productive place in life, and to regain the ability to begin new relationships. The goal is to complete the relationship with a loved one who has died, or a spouse or friend who has left, so that you can revisit the emotional relationship without all the pain attached. Loss is part of life; experience and common sense reveal that the longer you live, the more losses you will encounter.

<u>Losses Leading to Grief</u>

Grief can result from a great number of loss experiences. As a matter of fact, life can be looked at as a *series of losses*:

- when we are born, we lose the warm, secure environment of the womb;
- as we grow we lose our innocence;
- when we go to school, we must lose some of our dependence upon Mom;
- we get toys and teeth that we eventually lose;
- we lose pets;
- when we graduate from high school/college, we lose some of our acquaintances and friends;
- as we grow older we lose fitness, stamina, looks, health, etc.; and
- we lose loved ones.

In the midst of that series, other loss experiences include: marriage, financial changes, legal problems, moving, empty nest, holidays, and retirement.

The authors of *The Grief Recovery Handbook* state, "After twenty years of working with grievers, we have identified several other losses, including loss of trust, loss of safety, and loss of control of one's body (physical or sexual abuse). Society still does not recognize these losses as grief issues.[3] It is also important that we understand something about loss-of-trust events, because they are so prevalent in our culture. "Loss-of-trust events are experienced by almost everyone and can have a major, lifelong negative impact."[4]

Loss and the Believer

Many have lost trust in God or in people who represent God through the church. Christians may not recognize we register loss when we realize that our leaders and mentors aren't perfect. When congregations and denominations divide into factions, individuals grieve the loss of trust, sense of security, dreams, expectations, and community. When a pastor moves to another church, whatever the circumstance, loss is experienced in the entire community of faith.

Our response to God's desire for a fulfilling relationship is influenced by our image of God. If we've experienced disappointments, betrayals of trust, lack of approval, lack of affirmation, or lack of love, we may view God differently than people who were reared in a nurturing, secure environment. And even if we did feel secure and loved as a child, if we haven't dealt with the ordinary disappointments and losses of life, we'll have difficulty building a close connection with God.

Unprocessed loss impairs our ability to connect with other people and to God.

Many of us were encouraged to put the past behind us, look at the bright side, and not dwell on the negative. If so, we probably feel that we don't have any unprocessed losses. We're probably wrong! When we gloss over a disappointment, or loss of trust and security, or a grief, we may not think about it anymore, but the buried pain still exists. We shut off some of the rooms in our hearts. We begin to trust other people less and are slower to open our hearts. We lose some of our capacity for the joy that's available to us. Subsequently, we aren't truthful with ourselves, with others, or with God about our feelings.

Too many of us sit on the floor, eating crumbs, when the God of all creation wants us to feast with Him at the banquet table. We know from Scripture that God intends an amazing feast for us, but our hearts insist we aren't worthy, or that we can't trust Him to provide for us. So, in response, we try to pretend that the pain isn't there.

What's your heart crying out for? Perhaps you know and can articulate it. For others, the stirring is there, but they feel they lack the words or ability to express it. For others, a cold lifelessness has developed, and they yearn for fire and warmth.

Perhaps God has brought you through rivers you thought would drown you or fires you were certain would consume you. Now that you've survived and are on the other side, you still yearn for that joy unspeakable, that peace that surpasses all understanding. God wants to answer the deep yearning of your heart.

CHAPTER 2
EXPRESSING DISAPPOINTMENT
OR ANGER WITH GOD

God wants to guide you into a more intimate relationship with Him. You may be thinking: *That's the last thing I want right now. God hasn't been very good to me, and in fact, He's the last person I want to associate with right now!* Great! This book is for those who believe, those who are in a crisis of faith, and those who don't believe at all but are willing to consider another viewpoint.

One profound truth is that on planet Earth *all* of our relationships can end except the one we have with God. Hurricane Katrina, 9/11, war, and other acts of terrorism have already taken an emotional toll on the citizens of this country. We can look around the globe and easily see that loss comes with the territory.

Jesus, the King of Kings, came to lose His life, and yet, most of us, even his tried-and-true followers don't have any practical, emotional tools when we're faced with monumental losses. In the midst of our loss, if we refuse to or are not allowed to express those deep disappointments with God, we can find ourselves in a holding pattern where our spiritual growth is blocked. And, of course, if we're struggling with disappointment or anger with God in our own lives, how can we answer those tough questions when a church member comes to our office with those same questions: Why me? Why a child? Why the nice people? This is what God gives me after I spent my life serving Him? Our best answers, in such cases, are going to be rhetorical, spiritualized statements, which might be true, but do absolutely nothing to help grievers because they address the intellect and not the emotions.

When our emotions are like the lights on a flashing neon sign, it becomes quite difficult for us to connect with spiritual or intellectual statements. Such an onslaught of emotions has nothing to do with one's salvation or faith; it has everything to do with the way God chose to design human beings as emotional creatures.

For a moment, let's examine how broken human relationships lead to broken spiritual relationships. If your unfinished business includes anger with God, or a loss of trust in Him, you're certainly out of fellowship with Him. God wants you back. I hope that the tools in this book will help you finish your business with God and other people, so you can return to and deepen the intimate relationship He so desires to have with you.

Many of us who are in the midst of grave disappointment with God, not understanding why a family member wasn't healed or why an accident claimed an innocent life, have to know that it's alright and actually beneficial to express our feelings of anger and disappointment. Do not fear His wrath. Since God knows and searches our hearts, it's in our best interest to be transparent with our omniscient Creator. The following poem by Jessica Shaver captures the freedom that's available to believers who trust the Lord with their deepest emotions.

<u>I Told God I Was Angry</u>

I told God I was angry. I thought He'd be surprised. I thought I'd kept hostility quite cleverly disguised. I told the Lord I hate Him. I told Him that I hurt. I told Him that He isn't fair; He's treated me like dirt. I told God I was angry, but I'm the one surprised. "What I've known all along," He said, "you've finally realized." At last you have admitted what is really in your heart. Dishonesty, not anger, was keeping us apart. Even when you hate me, I don't stop loving you. Before you can receive that love, you must confess what's true. In telling me the anger you genuinely feel, it loses power over you, permitting you to heal. I told God I was sorry, and He's forgiven me. The truth that I was angry has finally set me free.[5]

Anger at another person, or at God, reflects our humanity, not our level of faith or devotion. And a lack of anger doesn't mean that we're at a "higher level" of faith than someone who does feel anger. Many of us have been so conditioned to suppress our anger that we're surprised to learn it's there, having been stuffed down during all the years we weren't allowed or invited to express it. If the anger is there, we'll find it in the process of Grief

Recovery® and "complete" it.

Unresolved grief, with the specific fruit of subconscious or conscious disappointment in God, seems to be blocking believers from deeply experiencing and enjoying intimacy with God. And because of loss-of-trust events, too many of us never completely trust God with our circumstances or lives. If we, as believers, were honest, many of us would acknowledge that we are too wounded to truly obey Jesus' invitation to "follow Him," and neither can we obey the first commandment to love God with *all* our heart, mind, soul, and strength. What a grievous state this is, for wounded believers, to the heart of God, and to the unsaved world who doesn't see us walking in His pure and powerful light.

CHAPTER 3
URGENT: CALL TO THE CHURCH

It's critical that we, as the body of Christ, come forth into the light of freedom and expose the darkness, so that we'll be prepared, positioned, and ready to stand strong as we enter into the last days. God is through with our "playing church," and now the question becomes one of putting our actions where our mouth is. God is saying, "If you love Me, hear My cries for transparency, and step up to the plate."

I, for one, don't want to answer to God someday why I didn't share what He had placed within me. That's why I'm writing this book. I would rather go to the dentist, than sit down and write, if that tells you anything! I gave God every excuse: I can't spell; I can't write; and on and on. But in my heart of hearts, I knew He wasn't going to let it go. I knew His patience would eventually run its course and He'd say, "Enough, I told you now is the day and the hour." I've experienced other times when God commands me to be His scribe.

On Friday, March 11, 2005, God woke me up at six a.m. and said, "Write." I picked up my pen, and like lightning it sailed across the page. As I watched the pen move, I had no clue what was being written. I was just trying to be an accurate stenographer. When I finished, the Lord immediately gave me instructions. I was to share this message with the one hundred and fifty bishops I would be addressing at the Annual Association of Pentecostal Bishops' Conference in Ohio the following week. Here is the Lord's message I delivered at nine a.m., Thursday, March 17, 2005:

"This is a new season. It is a time of cleansing and preparation for My Church to move into a position of authority over the powers of darkness. This is authority that you have not had in the past because Satan has blinded your eyes with intellectualism, but I am saying with love you shall conquer.

"What has been acceptable in the past will no longer be. There is a higher level of transparency required for this new season, for this new level I have called you to. Rise up and stand in the gap of the new door I am opening in your heart and in your mind. The veil is being removed. In the end times it is going to take a level of maturity to stand against the dark one. This is a battle, and you, my children, must rise up and be prepared for the battle. Your heart belongs to me, but you have been letting Satan have dominion in areas that perhaps you had no clue he was controlling. But I am taking away the scales from your eyes, so that you can press in and remove the scales from your heart. The time is now, and you must be prepared and ready to move into your new season. I am closing the doors of what you saw as intimacy with me in the past, and I am taking you to a new level, a level that you have never seen before, a level that will touch the world with love and power. And as you stand in the pulpit and speak truth from your heart, people will be drawn in, not by your intellectual prowess, but by the transparency of your heart.

As I began speaking, the presence of the Lord was so strong that all the bishops rose to their feet. Many were silently weeping. My pastor, Ed Langham, who'd just celebrated his fiftieth year as a minister (and who, as a Presbyterian, had probably never heard a prophetic word before) stood there with crocodile tears running down his face. When I moved into my lecture, people sat down, but it was clear: God's message had made an impact.

At the end of my second day of teaching, Bishop Alfred Owens, the Dean of the College of African-American Pentecostal Bishops, who previously had his misgivings about my "talking about feelings and dredging up the past ministry," came and thanked me profusely, saying it was just what the Church needs.

Part of my calling is to help heal and empower pastors, training them in Grief Recovery® techniques, so that they are better equipped to give real help to their hurting sheep. One of the most off-limit topics of conversation in the United States is grief. We don't have any problems talking about dying, death, sex, etc., but we shrink back from discussing grief. God wants to expose our unresolved loss, this silent killer in the church. We need to allow our Creator to examine our hearts with our cooperation, so we can walk in Sonship and also be the ready, spotless bride for whom He is returning.

.

CHAPTER 4
REMOVING THE SCALES
FROM OUR HEARTS

So many churches today have marquees that read: "Revival!" Each time I drive by one of these, I'm reminded that revival comes from a cleansing and healing of our hearts. We cannot skip that step. To be spotless, we have to invite God to enter our secret corridors.

Here are a few challenging questions to ask yourself: Am I willing to let God truly transform me to be more like Him, or am I merely going through the motions of religious activities? Part of that question involves looking deeply and honestly into our daily walk. Are we happy to be done with our evening devotionals, so we can sit back and watch a movie or a ball game? Do we wake up and meet with the King of Kings, our Commander-in-Chief, to hear our daily instructions? Or do we wake up and think about coffee and feel rushed to put the kids on the school bus before we're late for work?

How many times in a day do we pause before

speaking or acting to listen to God's promptings? If Jesus only said and did what His Father said and did, are we only doing and saying what God is instructing? When is the last time God spoke to your spirit? What did He say? How can we be transformed if we're not listening? How can we obey if we're unfamiliar with His loving voice? Jesus said His sheep hear His voice.

If you're feeling convicted right now that you haven't loved the Lord your God with *all* your heart, soul, and mind, let's examine possible reasons why. What are those things taking up space in your heart? Our God is a jealous God; His tabernacle is our heart, and He doesn't want to share His dwelling place with fear, anger, shame, bitterness, unforgiveness, emotional wounds, or an unwillingness (to move out from our comfort zone).

Anything that comes between you and God blocks the union and communion for which you were created. Have you forsaken your first love for pain? For things of the world: TV, secular movies, or electronic games? For escape: music, drugs, alcohol, pornography, sex? For Christian pursuits: Bible studies, endless fellowship opportunities/activities, or religious conferences? When you need comfort, what or whom do you turn to first: your trusted friend, your spouse, your TV, your iPod, your refrigerator?

The human heart, not the intellect, is the driving force of an intimate relationship with Christ. In your heart is where you find your Lover. I have heard it said that Jesus is the only Bridegroom whose Bride barely talks with Him. Yet, He's the only one who can renew and restore your heart. His *rhema* (living word) brings the deepest kind of healing that, no matter how anointed, no human can facilitate.

When a diamond is first brought out of the mine, it's covered with black carbon. Once the carbon is chipped away, the diamond's true nature is revealed, and its brilliant, sparkling facets can be clearly seen. We're like diamonds. Each of our hearts was created perfect, "in His likeness."

As our responses to circumstances of our lives produced carbon around our hearts, the beautiful jewel within lost luster, beauty, and was finally obscured altogether. Thankfully, God can see the diamond beneath the carbon, even if we, and the people around us, are unable to comprehend the jewel concealed beneath the layers. God wants to help us chip away those layers, to clearly "see with our hearts" all the legitimacy and power He's given us as believers.

It's my burning desire, and the burning desire of so many in the church, that the body of Christ be shed of these layers of carbon, so that all of us can be drawn into a more intimate relationship with the Father, where we are free and joyous, so the church can be all that it was created to be, so others will want what we have, and so we can make a difference in the world. Then we can glorify God and make Him smile!

Before discussing Grief Recovery® as a solution to the silent killer in the church, I need to more fully illustrate the problem. As we all know, many believers, as well as unbelievers, see the church as a dysfunctional institution. I believe the problem lies in man's unresolved grief and lack of emotional skills. God's love and healing power is still available to those who diligently seek Him, but many of us are listening to social, intellectual, and spiritual lies.

I recently interviewed Bishop Joey Johnson who's been a pastor for over thirty years. His church, House of the Lord, in Akron, Ohio, averages about 1800 people for Sunday services. He sees a major problem in the community of Christ. Believers tend not to deal with loss, and leaders, too, don't want to face their own pain, which he refers to as "theology suffering." He and his staff have been looking at why the people who come to church don't seem to get any better. People drop into a "faith crisis" when God doesn't cure them of their physical and emotional issues. They believe in God, but they're feeling guilty for "not having enough faith," for "not praying enough," or for "not fasting enough."

The bishop and his staff believe that the Christian community as a whole may not truly see God, that deep inside, they may have a problem with Him, which impacts their emotions and systems of thought. People, he said, want a "quick fix," but they need to be more cognizant that there's *God's part* and *our part* in the process of healing.

Too often, however, people's pain blocks them from hearing God, the voice of their comforter and healer. It's also evident that many pastors are suffering from "compassion fatigue." They desperately want to help their flock, but they and others are in desperate need of workable tools.

Acting Healed Syndrome

Wherever I go, I ask people to raise their hands if they've been grieving for over twenty years. Always, hands go up. Our society tends to think of grief as something people feel for a short while after a major loss. Time, they're told, heals all things, so whether one's grief has lessened or not, one must put on a "coping face" after a while. Lie #1 is that time heals grief. The "acting recovered syndrome" shows up so often in our churches. We're urged to view adversity from a positive angle. It's common for pastors to say, "Remember, your flesh should be crucified! You should be *dead* to your feelings!" Let's understand that the "sensuality of the flesh," is very, very different from pain that registers in the "heart"! No pastor would feel too comfortable with saying, "Your heart should be dead!" But that's what so many are saying, albeit in different words.

Friends and church leaders often exhort us to find joy in the Lord in *all* aspects of life. Such words encourage us to "act recovered," especially around our church friends, and if we don't appear "recovered" in what some Christians consider a reasonable time frame, they'll be praying for our soul. A clear example of this occurs in the book of Job. As long as his friends sat silently and shared his sorrow, they were a comfort. Once they opened their mouths, however, their searing indictments only compounded Job's suffering.

They Spiritualize

Often Christians unwittingly try to "spiritualize away" pain. Others may indicate that if we were closer to God, we wouldn't suffer as much from our sorrow. They give us pat spiritual comments without understanding the negative impact of their words:

- "He's in a better place."

- "If you have enough faith. . . "

- "Just give it to God."

- "All things work together for good."

- "Keep your eyes on Jesus, and everything will be okay."

- "The Lord giveth, and the Lord taketh away."

- "The Lord will not give you more than you can bear."

- "Pray more."

- "Read the Bible more."

- "Deny self."

- "Death doesn't matter to Christians."

- "He's with Jesus."

- "Let go and let God."

It's reassuring that we have God's infinite resources for strength. In times of deep grieving, however, our emotions may so overwhelm us that we may not be able to utilize these resources. Then we begin to feel guilty for a lack of faith, in addition to the other, conflicting emotions that churn within us.

We need to experience the natural range of human emotions that accompany loss. When our emotions are going on and off like a neon sign, they distract us and inhibit our ability to hear or to connect with those spiritual tools we hold so dear. We can become confused and question why these familiar methods aren't working. It's at this point that many begin to doubt their faith, thinking, *Something must be wrong with me spiritually.*

Grievers note that devotional times, particular services, or music that normally comforts them, seem meaningless. They often report the sensation that their prayers "hit the ceiling and fall back down."

Many confess feeling they feel removed from the presence of God. They call to Him, but feel He doesn't hear.

This breaks our Heavenly Father's heart that we're taught to "spiritualize" our grief away, rather than deal with the emotions associated with the loss. This lack of help and concurrent wounding leads us to feel further isolated from the very community that should provide the most comfort to us. This is why I believe unresolved grief is the hidden killer in the institutional church.

When my former husband and I divorced, church leaders discussed whether or not I could continue to teach Sunday school and serve as president of the Women's Mission Group. At a time when I most needed support and compassion, I felt judged and abandoned. My loss was not acknowledged by church members; they never mentioned the divorce.

The Tragedy

The Christian community could be a wonderful support system to chip away the carbon around our grieving members' hearts, but too often it's not. Too many Christians don't know how to heal their own pain, much less reach out to others.

My files are filled with the pain and hurt clients experience from those who represent the church. One case in point: Jim and Susan had given up their life of comfort to pursue a life of serving Christ as missionaries. Their resources were stretched, trying to care for three children, aged ten, eleven, and thirteen. They'd traveled to another state to be interviewed for a possible church position, and the next day, on their way home, they decided to stop at the beach, so the children could play in the water.

While Jim and Susan sat on the shoreline conversing, they watched their youngsters joyfully playing in the ocean. Suddenly, they heard a cry no parent ever wants to hear, and Jim rushed out into the water to try and rescue his youngest son. But it was too late. Just as he reached him, the tide sucked the little boy out to sea. It took the rescue team over an hour to recover his body.

The heartbroken family returned to the pastor's home where they'd been the previous evening. As the word spread, people from the church began arriving at the pastor's home to pay their condolences to the family. We can only imagine how distraught Jim was over the death of his son and not being able to save him! So, as a normal reaction to all this, he had tears running down his face. The pastor nudged him. "Jim, dry your face and stop crying. If the people see you crying, they'll think that you have no faith." That was the first of many cruel events this family experienced from "the church."

Jim and Susan's son had been in a group that occasionally sang *a cappella* in their church. One Sunday evening, several months later, the group performed for the congregation. As Jim sat there listening, the tears started to flow as the memories returned. The man sitting next to Jim's wife asked, "What's wrong with Jim?"

Linda answered, "Don't you remember our son used to sing in this group?"

The man replied, "Isn't he over it yet?!"

I wish that I could say that was the end of the cruel treatment for this family, but I can't. The last and final thing I know that made it clear them that they wouldn't receive help from their church leadership came from their pastor. Jim and Linda had come to my Grief Recovery® Outreach Program which met on Thursday evenings. For the first time since their son died, they felt someone was hearing and acknowledging their pain. When Jim told his pastor that he'd be attending a Grief Recovery® group on Thursday evenings for the next eight weeks, the pastor replied, "Jim, you can't do that because we have visitation on Thursday evenings, and that has to come first."

Here was a couple who'd given up everything to serve God, and not only did they lose their child, but they consequently experienced such deep pain and rejection from the very place that was supposed to be a sanctuary for the hurting. What a tragedy!

What happened to this family is not uncommon; there's a multitude of ways that the hurt and grieving aren't invited to heal as a result of well-meant, but very wrong, responses. My passion to bring Grief Recovery® education to as many church leaders as possible has been fueled by the fact that my files are full of cases where those who represent the church have wounded grievers more than they have helped them.

Dwight L. Carlson examines this irony in his book, *Why Do Christians Shoot Their Wounded?* He writes, "I have found that many not only deny problems but are intolerant of those with emotional difficulties. Many judge that others' emotional problems are the direct result of personal sin. At any one time, up to fifteen percent of our population is experiencing significant emotional problems. For them our churches need to be sanctuaries of healing, not places where they must hide their wounds."[7]

In his book, *Naked and Not Ashamed*, T.D. Jakes so eloquently asks the question, "Can you hear the hollow moans of sheep who bleed behind the stained glass and upon the padded pew?"[8] Far too many people sit on the church pew with pious faces while they're emotionally bleeding to death. They're consciously or subconsciously thinking, *I don't want you to know of my pain because you might reject me for not having enough faith. If you knew the depth of my sorrow, you might decide I don't have an adequate spiritual foundation.* Other thoughts might be, *Why am I having all these problems, and Ellen's life is wonderful? I know she loves the Lord, but I love Him, too, so there must be something wrong with me. Maybe I'm not really that spiritual.*

This fear of rejection or judgment reveals an alarming lack of emotional support for believers. In fact, John James, co-author of *The Grief Recovery Handbook* heard a heart-breaking statistic at an Ohio Methodist's Bishops' Conference in the mid '80s. It was reported that after a significant emotional loss, church members will return to church three to four times. If their emotional needs are not met, fifty-two percent will never return. And we wonder why people in our country are leaving organized churches by the droves.

Ask God How to Help

According to our Bible, we are sheep who are supposed to hearken our Shepherd's voice, so it should go without saying that all of us need to ask God during our private prayer time about what we can do to help a particular lost or grieving sheep in our midst. We must now assume what that person needs. The Lord might tell you to just be a "heart with ears" (imagine yourself with tape over your mouth), or He might tell you to do nothing but pray a particular Psalm, or He might tell you to give them a gift card to a particular pizza franchise, so they can order in pizza during those nights when cooking for the kids seems overwhelming. One woman, whose teenage son was killed in a car accident, reported that one of the most inspired condolence cards she received contained coupons for free pizzas and a gift card to Blockbuster. Some nights that was exactly what she and her family needed. We're to extend to our brothers and sisters

Jesus' love, and He came to heal the broken hearted, not to throw stones at them.

Keeping Busy: Just a Distraction

Another lie that the church perpetuates is that keeping busy helps dissipate a griever's pain. But here is an important question: Does keeping busy *discover* and *complete* the pain caused by loss? The obvious answer is no. Then what does keeping busy accomplish, if anything? It's a distraction. It makes one more day go by. Churches have an endless supply of good works to keep the grieving Christian busy. Many church-goers believe that "an idle mind is the devil's workshop" and urge grievers to keep the devil at bay with a staggering array of service opportunities.

Some of us find it difficult to overcome the possibility that if we'd been good enough, prayed enough, or summoned up enough faith, God wouldn't have let this tragedy happen. We can feel guilty and blame ourselves that we didn't rise up to be stronger warriors in the spirit. When this kind of guilt sets in, it might help to recall Webster's simple definition of guilt: "The state of one who has committed an offense, especially consciously."[9] So if we had no intent to cause harm, we're not guilty.

Other people hop from one church to another, rather than dealing with unresolved emotional issues within those congregations, thus replacing the loss, but not resolving the problem. Some people hop from women's group to women's group or charity to charity. Men, too, can join a slew of men's groups or Bible studies and still not find any deep, emotional help.

CHAPTER 5
EMOTIONS NEED EXPRESSION!

According to James and Friedman, "Grief is the conflicting feelings caused by the end or change in a familiar pattern of behavior."[10] And it's the normal and natural reaction to loss of any kind.[11] Grief is not a behavior but an emotion, and as complex human beings, we have varied emotional reactions to loss. One size does not fit all. It's also important to remember that if a relationship has been difficult and it ends, a griever is still left with all the unmet hopes of someday repairing or making the relationship different. It's in the context of, "Now, nothing can be done. . ." that unresolved emotions reside. Difficult or estranged relationships don't hurt any less.

We must also understand that feelings and emotions are natural, and that stuffing them down is unnatural and destructive mentally, physically, and spiritually. In *the Cry of the Soul,* the authors so eloquently remind us:

"Ignoring our emotions is turning our back on

reality. Listening to our emotions ushers us into reality. And reality is where we meet God. . . Emotions ...are the language of the soul. They are the cry that gives the heart a voice. . . . However, we often turn a deaf ear--through emotional denial, distortion, or disengagement. We strain out anything disturbing in order to gain tenuous control of our inner world. We are frightened and ashamed of what leaks into our consciousness. In neglecting our intense emotions, we are false to ourselves and lose a wonderful opportunity to know God. We forget that change comes through brutal honesty and vulnerability before God.[12]

We have an excellent role model in Jesus for honestly expressing emotions as they occur. When He encountered merchants desecrating the Temple, He overturned the tables in rage. When He stood at the tomb of His friend Lazarus, He wept. When He contemplated death by crucifixion, He sweated "as drops of blood" and implored God to find another way. When He faced death, He cried, "My God, My God, why have You forsaken Me?" If our Savior experienced and expressed His emotions, and He was sinless and abided in His Heavenly Father, then surely expressing our emotions is acceptable in God's sight.

Don't Feel Bad Messages

Too many people want the comfort associated with spirituality, but not the risk and challenge that is par for the course for true followers of Jesus. Out of our own fear or discomfort, we don't want to engage with a griever's pain. Instead, we offer up the same platitudes that were given to us. I advise people to try not to say things like: "I know how you feel"; "Be strong for others"; "Be grateful he didn't suffer long"; "Keep busy"; "She led a full life"; "It must have been God's will"; "Don't you think you should be over it by now?"; "Just give it a little more time"; or "He wouldn't want you to waste time feeling bad, so just move on with your life." These statements shut down communication. They reveal poor listening skills, and they don't acknowledge the griever's unique feelings of loss.

It's so much wiser and better to pray and ask God if there's something comforting He wants to say through you. The Holy Spirit inside of us is our *Paraclete,* our Comforter, so let's remember that He's the one who can help us do and say what would truly be comforting! Saying or doing the simple things God instructs can go a very long way in helping someone engulfed in sorrow. It can help the griever summon up the determination to sit in God's presence, knowing that God really does want to communicate and heal.

Too many of us have been taught that feeling sad is bad. Instead of being taught to embrace and resolve our sorrow, we've had our emotions and feelings trivialized; unfortunately, this usually happens with those who love us most. Such trivializing of feelings and emotions is mostly unintentional, and occurs because of a lack of education. We then pass on what we've learned, not realizing the impact of our statements and how they send the message that we shouldn't have sad feelings. Yet we experience sad feelings anyway, and begin to think there's something wrong with us for having them.

Here are some commonly used statements that illustrate how we send "don't feel bad" messages and discount the person's feelings by our responses.

Relating To Pet Loss:

Don't feel bad – On Saturday we will get you a new dog.

Don't feel bad – It was only a dog (or cat, etc.)

Relating To Death:

Don't feel bad – She's in a better place.

Don't feel bad – His suffering is over.

Don't feel bad – It's just God's will.

Don't feel bad – You did everything you could.

Don't feel bad – Grandpa's in heaven.

Relating to Divorce or Romantic Breakup:

Don't feel bad – There are plenty of fish in the sea.

He or she wasn't right for you. It was just puppy love (especially said to teenagers).

Relating to Children of Divorcing Parents:

Don't feel bad; this isn't your fault.

Mommy and Daddy will have more time for you.

Mommy and Daddy still love you.

You'll have two of every holiday and birthday (at Mom's house and again at Dad's house).[13]

Even if you've experienced a similar loss, never say, "I know how you feel." It's an untrue statement. You couldn't possibly know how someone else feels because every relationship is unique. By making this statement, you discount the other person's feelings and the uniqueness of that relationship. You might offer, "I can't imagine how crushed your heart is, but when I lost my husband, I felt like my heart had been run over by a bulldozer. I felt like I couldn't even breathe for months." This kind of communication lets the other person know that you are willing to hear about *their* emotions without assuming your situations or feelings are identical.

Does Your Theology Block Healing?

Let me make this clear: theological faith (head knowledge) does not equate with emotional truth (heart knowledge). We know a multitude of things in our head, but do we believe them in our heart? Surely, in your mind, you believe God is who He says He is, that He can do what He says He can do, that You are a child of God, that you can do all things through Christ, that God's word is alive and active in you. But do you truly believe these words in your *heart*? There's a difference in believing in God and believing Him!

For too long the church has been developing into a Body that has been driven to acquire knowledge, details, facts, history, and numbers, and in this effort, somewhere along the way, we've missed the importance of the heart's role in true intimacy with God. Knowledge does not bring intimacy; it brings knowledge, and at best it brings an intellectual understanding. But it does not bring a heart knowledge or heart understanding.

Do we believe with our hearts that Jesus healed us on the cross? Our minds know this is true, but why are so many of us still brokenhearted? Instead of feeling ashamed, confused, or not spiritually worthy, we need to understand that our Almighty is a God of true love. Because of His desire for true intimacy, He offers you a gift: a deeper level of healing. He is always calling us deeper and higher. Therefore, we should have the willingness to let Him lead us, opening our hearts to the perfect and individual way He heals each of our hearts.

Our responsibility in our healing is to lift up our hammers and picks and start working with Father God (and others He brings into our lives to help). We join Him in chipping away the "carbon buildup" we have on the good hearts He has so graciously redeemed for us! It's time to admit that the modern church hasn't given us the tools to plunge into what St. John of the Cross called "the dark night of the soul." We need to confess that most of us are not living up to our potential, position, or power that we possess as believers.

Theologically, we know our position, but so often our *hearts* do not believe it. The Bible says we are meant to see with the eyes of our heart. That vision, according to God, is more real than what we see with our physical eyes. Our hearts were created to be open, but through a series of loss events (many of which involve trust), we began to close down those rooms in our heart in an effort to protect ourselves from future pain. Consequently, we can become caught up in hiding a related sin: fear—which comes when we dread any kind of loss.

The Bible says that when Jesus comes back, He will first judge His church. If you've had it up to your eyeballs with the hypocrisy, double standards, cruel pat answers, judgmental and arrogant attitudes of many who work in and represent the church, then imagine how God, in his long-suffering, all-encompassing love, feels. It's breaking His heart.

Life in Christ is about freedom, not bondage; joy, not coping; and peace, not anxiety and worries. How many of you at this moment can say, "I feel joyful and free"? What have we become slaves to? It's much easier to identify the material things we've become slaves to, but what about the interior voices that control our thoughts, actions, relationships, and our spiritual journeys? My goal here is not to condemn the modern church, but to uncover the darkness and prepare a path for the light of God's truth. God loves to move into a realm of darkness, stir it up, and then birth the light of His grace.

CHAPTER 6
THE BIBLE: A BOOK ABOUT HEARTS

I'm totally convinced that if Christians grasp hold of the truth that our redeemed hearts are new, clean, good, and not desperately wicked as so many well-meaning preachers have taught for the past one hundred years, our lives would be radically altered and reflect the transforming power of God's glory in our world. The problem began when the verse from Jeremiah 17:9, "The heart is deceitfully wicked" was applied to New Testament followers of Jesus Christ. This verse applies to unbelievers and those under the legal system of the Old Testament.

This "wicked heart theology" has discounted, demeaned, misconstrued, misrepresented, and wounded our hearts. The lie has become the stronghold that Satan uses to keep us from our "true and good hearts." Also, this theology has caused Christians to neglect the care of their hearts. To say that followers of Jesus have wicked hearts puts us in a position to live a divided life, a life that's in constant battle because peace has no place to reside.

When a person is born again, where does the Holy Spirit takes up residence? If the answer is the heart, then what kind of tabernacle is that, if the heart is *still* desperately wicked and not to be trusted? Can the third Person of the Trinity reside within an evil domain? If the heart continues to be desperately wicked after salvation, why does God's inspired Word say to "watch over your heart with all diligence, for from it flow the springs of life"?[14] Why would God tell us to protect and guard something that's so wicked?

In the explanation of the different types of soil, Jesus states that the good soil, which receives the seed of His Word, consists of those who have an "honest and good heart."[15] Where does that leave Jeremiah 17:9? Isn't it obvious that there are two distinctly different groups of people with distinctly different kinds of hearts?

Ezekiel speaks prophetically about the condition of the heart of New Testament believers when he declares that the Lord will give a new heart to His people, a heart that's able to be moved by His love.[16] Redeemed by our Savior, our heart contains our spiritual DNA and God's DNA. This establishes in us an unquenchable desire to want what He wants. What's important to Him becomes important to us. Our new default setting is a desire to walk with our Heavenly Father.

According to Dr. William P. Cheshire, Jr., Assistant Professor of Neurology at Mayo Medical School, there's physical evidence to support the scriptural assertion that God wrote His name on our hearts. After studying Hebrew for several years, he was busy at work one day, looking at films from an angiography when he first saw the connection. As he placed a magnetic resonance image of a cross-section of a human heart on the view box, he noticed how the outlines of the heart make a perfect *shin* (pronounced "sheen"), a Hebrew letter which, according to Hebrew scholars, commonly denotes one of Almighty God's Hebrew names: *El Shaddai*.

Dr. Cheshire also had new revelation of the two heart sounds that can be heard when listening through a stethoscope; the first is "sh . . . sh . . . sh . . . sh. . ," and the second is "dada . . . dada." These two sounds also approximated *El Shaddai*.[17] Our very breathing is an awesome picture of King David's words, "Let everything that has breath praise the Lord." All day and all night long, until we die, our bodies inhale and exhale the name of our Sovereign God!

Unfortunately, not understanding the true, resonating image of our hearts leads us to desire and long for the things of the world. Our heart's thirsting can *only* be quenched by following the desires God puts in our hearts. Invite Him in to heal your image of your heart and work in unison with Him in chipping away its carbon walls. Then you will be able to keep the commandment to love your Lord with all of your heart. Then we Christians will be able to clearly see, understand, and succeed in our role with Jesus as co-healers of human hearts.

<u>The Heart of the Matter</u>

The Bible is a book mostly concerned with the heart, not the head. It's written mostly by Jews, in the context of a Hebraic society and culture. Even the New Testament, although written in *Koine*

Greek, the common language of the people during the time of Christ, was still immersed in Hebraic teachings and understandings. As a people entrusted with the Scriptures, the Jews were much more concerned with concepts like the heart, soul, and spirit than the Greeks, who with their humanistic understandings, were much more concerned with concepts like the mind, intellect, and thoughts.

Significantly, it's *not* the Hebrew mindset, but the Greek mindset that's heavily influenced America, and the impact of the Enlightenment and Greek thinking upon American thought and theology has promoted an elevating of thoughts over feelings. Furthermore, I have heard it taught that a territorial spirit called the Prince of Greece (mentioned in Daniel 10:20), has a great deal of influence over America.

In the United States, most preaching is done with a Greek mindset, assuming spiritual truths can be received in the mind instead of the heart and human spirit. We would do well to remember Paul's words, "For indeed Jews ask for signs and *Greeks search for wisdom*; but we preach Christ crucified, to Jews a stumbling block and to Gentiles foolishness. . . " (emphasis mine).[18] Paul also wrote, "And when I came to you, brethren, I did not come with superiority of speech or of wisdom, proclaiming to you the testimony of God. For I determined to know nothing among you except Jesus Christ and Him crucified. I was with you in weakness and in fear and in much trembling, and my message and my preaching were not in persuasive words of wisdom, but in demonstration of the Spirit and of power, so that our faith would not rest on the wisdom of men, but on the power of God."[19]

Spiritual truth is not apprehended through rational thought, which is not to say that our brains are irrelevant in processing spiritual truth. They're just a facet for understanding, encountering, or communing with God.

The word "heart" is mentioned 725 times in the Old Testament and 105 times in the New Testament, for a total of 830 times altogether. It is noteworthy that "mind" only appears 157 times in the entire Bible.[21] Why do you think that is? The answer is that God is a Supreme Being who's after our hearts (where love emanates), and the wisest of us should be like David, who despite his sins and mistakes, spent his life seeking after God's own heart.

So what is really meant by the word "heart"? The *New International Dictionary of New Testament Theology* offers an excellent definition: "However, in its abstract meanings, "heart" became the richest biblical term for the totality of man's inner or immaterial nature. In biblical literature it is the most frequently used term for man's immaterial personality functions as well as the most inclusive term for them, since, in the Bible, virtually every immaterial function of man is attributed to the "heart."[20]

In short, in biblical terms, a "heart" is the totality of the intellect, emotions, and will. There can be no life-transforming encounter with God except through the heart and the human spirit, which is the heart of the heart.

Love the God of Your Heart

Believers must always remember that our Creator is a jealous God; Jesus stated that the greatest commandment was to: ". . . love the Lord your God with all your heart, soul, and mind."[21] In other words, He doesn't want roommates in the tabernacle of our hearts! It's time to kick out all those other inhabitants.

One's heart encompasses the physical organ, a person's inner feelings, as well as one's deepest thoughts and understandings. It can be considered the place of emotions.

Here's another urgent warning, "Be on guard that your hearts may not be weighted down with dissipation and drunkenness and the worries of life, and that day come on you suddenly like a trap."[22] We can't hide our hearts from God because He created them, His name is upon them, and He judges us by them. Consider the following verse: "I, the LORD, search the heart, I test the mind, even to give to each man according to his ways, according to the results of his deeds."[23] God sees with piercing eyes, looking through all outward appearances to examine our innermost being. The writer of Hebrews makes this point absolutely clear:

"For the word of God is living and active and sharper than any two-edged sword, and piercing as far as the division of soul and spirit, of both joints and marrow, and able to judge the thoughts and intentions of the heart. And there is no creature hidden from His sight, but all things are open and laid bare to the eyes of Him with whom we have to do."[24]

Since God "knows the secrets" of our hearts (Ps. 44:21) and He wants us to pour out our heart to Him (Ps. 62:8), shouldn't we accept the fact that our hearts are what matter *most* to Him? Our Lord wants the peace of Christ to rule in our hearts (Col. 3:15); He wants our hearts pure and undivided (Ps. 86:11); and He promises to strengthen the hearts of those who love Him (2 Chron. 16:9).

There's no fooling the God who searches our deepest thoughts and desires (Heb. 4:12) and wants us to know Him (by following His promptings in the radical, abiding way that Jesus did and said we could). We must allow Him to dwell in our heart.

So, what's the problem? The problem is that most of us are consciously or subconsciously intimidated by intimacy. We've been so impacted by the Enlightenment, Rationalism, Modernism, and the Greek-oriented modes of thinking that we've seriously minimized the emotional and spiritual aspects of humanity. We've so minimized these aspects of existence that we've become uncomfortable with and intimidated by them. For the church to move into the place that God wants us to be, we'll need to change our paradigm to see that Christianity is relationship-centered, not reason-centered.

- Christianity is *not* a set of theological propositions.
- Christianity is *not* doctrine.
- Christianity is *not* intellectual knowledge.
- Christianity is *not* a set of rules.

Christianity is a loving, trusting relationship with God the Father, Jesus Christ, and the Holy

Spirit! Let's consider a very powerful word from Almighty God, "And you will seek Me and find Me, when you search for Me with *all your heart*" (emphasis mine).[25]

Too many of us can't bring the emotions of our hearts to God, because our hearts are walled off. Peter Scazzero explains a key step in fixing this situation: "Paul teaches in 2 Corinthians 5:17 that when we become Christians, old things pass away and all things become new. But crisis taught me I had to go back and understand what those old things were in order for them to begin passing away."[26]

Sadly, when we become Christians, we're not taught to go back and understand what the "old things" are, so that we can identify them and take the steps to be free of old habit structures and patterns of relating.

For the old things to pass away, they need to be identified, acknowledged, and grieved. How can you let go of something if you're not certain about what it is you're holding onto? For many of us, we've been taught that we need to "let sleeping dogs lie" and "keep the past in the past." "Why dig up old bones?" we're asked. "Just move on!" God created us in His image as processing plants not storage tanks. Processing plants filter out what is toxic to make what remains clean and viable. Storage tanks only become dirtier and more defiled if they're not regularly and thoroughly cleaned. The past still affects our present and future if we lack the skills to identify, acknowledge, and grieve past hurts, disappointments, and unmet dreams.

Repent for a Hardened Heart

Grief Recovery® provides a practical step-by-step process to discover that which is hidden. While a wonderful tool, when it's combined with the loving, revelatory light of the Holy Spirit, it will then equip you to reach into those deep, dark places. Awareness becomes the first step in the process of discovering that which is hidden or emotionally unfinished.

In repenting for his adultery with Bathsheba and the murder of her husband, David wrote, "Create in me a clean heart, O God, and renew a steadfast spirit within me."[27] Before God can clean our hearts, the hardened walls that surround them must come down. King David warned his people, "Do not harden your hearts, as at Meribah, as in the day of Massah in the wilderness."[28] When the Israelites traveled through the wilderness and found no water to drink, the people quarreled with Moses, demanding that he provide water. Moses asked them why they were acting this way, and why they tested the Lord, in their questioning of His divine presence among them.

Ignoring his words, the people continued to complain, and the Lord told Moses to stand in front of them and strike the rock at Horeb, so that water might come out of it for the people to drink. Moses obeyed, but he named the place *Massah* ("burden") and *Meribah* ("provocation" and "strife").[29] The Israelites hardness of heart caused the Israelites to repeatedly test the Lord and not listen to His voice.

It's tragic how the same thing is happening to His people today. We know God is with us, performing miracles all over the world, but the hardness of our hearts keeps so many of us from walking in that same power. Even after Jesus miraculously fed the five thousand, an amazing miracle, they failed to discern a spiritual principle, "For they had not gained any insight from the incident of the loaves, but their heart was hardened."[30] Hardness of the heart was also seen in the issue of divorce: "Some Pharisees came up to Jesus, testing Him, and began to question Him whether it was lawful for a man to divorce a wife. And He answered and said to them, "What did Moses command you?" They said, "Moses permitted a man to write a certificate of divorce and send her away." But Jesus said to them, "Because of *your hardness of heart* he wrote you this commandment" (emphasis mine).[31]

Moses had only permitted the Israelites to divorce their wives because of their hardness of heart, not because it conveyed the perfect will of God. Hardness of heart was a problem, even for Jesus' chosen disciples: "Afterward He appeared to the eleven as they were reclining at the table; and He reproached them for their unbelief and hardness of heart, because they had not believed those who had seen Him after He had risen."[32]

Their hard hearts kept the remaining disciples (Judas had already committed suicide) from believing the report that He had risen!

Paul also addresses the problem in Romans: "Or do you think lightly of the riches of His kindness and tolerance and patience, not knowing that the kindness of God leads you to repentance? But because of your stubbornness and unrepentant heart you are storing up wrath for yourself in the day of wrath and revelation of the righteous judgment of God."[33]

You might be thinking, *I don't see the phrase "hardness of heart" in these verses?* You're right. This updated New American Standard version translates the Greek word (*sklerotes*) as "stubbornness," but the King James version translates the word as "hardness." It's also interesting that Paul coupled impenitence, a lack of repentance, with "hardness." So, we can conclude that "hardness of heart" also implies an unrepentant heart!

According to the previous verse, if a hard and unrepentant heart is a problem, the answer must be the opposite: a soft or repentant heart. I want to take this one step further. I believe the answer is deep repentance. I believe there's a major difference between deep repentance and shallow repentance.

Shallow vs. Deep Repentance

Deep repentance penetrates the intellect, emotions, and will; shallow repentance does not. David experienced deep repentance over his sin with Bathsheba, while Esau experienced shallow repentance with respect to selling his birthright. Esau's experience is summed up in Hebrews:

"See to it that no one comes short of the grace of God; that no root of bitterness springing up causes trouble, and by it many be defiled; that there be no immoral or godless person like Esau who sold his own birthright for a single meal. For you know that even afterwards, when he desired to inherit the blessing, he was rejected, for he found no place for repentance, though he sought for it with tears."[34]

I believe that Esau didn't approach repentance with *all of his heart*, even though he sought for it with tears. Godly sorrow must penetrate every facet of the heart! Tears can be a sign of godly sorrow, but tears alone do not necessarily indicate a deeply repentant heart. Some people cry because they're exposed, not because they are genuinely sorry that they've broken the heart of God.

I would define deep repentance as a decision to turn from sin based upon a true change of heart. In David's repentance, He begged God for a clean heart. The Old Testament refers to this clean heart and renewed spirit as a "circumcised heart." As the foreskin of the male sexual organ is cut away, which allows it to be more potent in planting seed and creating life, so the foreskin of the heart needs to be cut away, so that it can be more potent in planting spiritual seed and creating spiritual life. Remember how Moses exhorted the Israelites, "So circumcise your heart, and stiffen your neck no longer."[35]

God gives similar words through Jeremiah: "Circumcise yourselves to the Lord and remove the foreskins of your heart, men of Judah and inhabitants of Jerusalem, or else My wrath will go forth like fire and burn with none to quench it, because of the evil of your deeds."[36] On a daily basis, we should do as David, the man after God's own heart, who boldly asked for his own heart to be fully revealed, "Search me, O God, and know my heart; try me and know my anxious thoughts; and see if there be any hurtful way in me, and lead me in the everlasting way."[37]

David was also unafraid of expressing his feelings to his Creator. Many have noted that the

Psalms mention virtually every known human feeling or emotion! David, although a mighty king, was less successful as a father. He was well-acquainted with losses, which kept him constantly relying on God to ease his parental sorrows. Knowing where our losses began, and understanding that they didn't originate with us, helps put the concept of deep repentance into a larger context.

The First Loss Event: The Fall of Adam and Eve

With the Fall of Adam and the entrance of sin into the stream of humanity, there came into being loss events, and something happened to our hearts. Sin is a loss event in and of itself, and sin precipitates all other loss events. All loss events flow from the very first loss event. What losses did Adam and Eve experience?

- Loss of intimacy with God.
- Loss of intimacy with each other.
- Loss of intimacy or consistency with self (disassociation).
- Loss of balance: spirit, soul, and body living in perfect unity.
- Loss of their home (The Garden of Eden).
- Loss of security.
- Loss of significance.
- Loss of innocence.
- Loss of trust.
- Loss of eternal life (death came into the world).

Ultimately, these losses hardened Adam and Eve's hearts, and all of humanity was impacted.

How Did God Handle Loss?

Let's examine how God handled His losses in connection with the same loss. He *grieved* that He had created humanity! In Genesis we read, "And the Lord was sorry that He had made man on the earth, and He was *grieved in His heart* (italics mine)."[38] How did God handle his grief?

How? Well, first God acknowledged His grief as well as the problematic situation. Second, He not only made preparations to forgive Adam and Eve of their sins, He also began the process of forgiving and redeeming humanity. "The Lord God made garments of skin for Adam and his wife, and clothed them."[39] We assumed that God killed the animals for those skins so that they could be "covered," the sacrificed animal skins foreshadowing the Lamb of God. Yet Adam and Eve were forgiven, looking forward to the cross, just as we are saved, looking back at the cross. We also see that the Almighty we serve doesn't hold grudges against the repentant; He embraces them with open arms!

Jesus Modeled Grief and Other Emotions

Grief is a biblical concept, and the three members of the Godhead grieve and work through their grief. Jesus ". . . was despised and forsaken of men, a man of sorrows, and acquainted with grief; and like one from whom men hide their faces, He was despised, and we did not esteem Him."[40] And how can we forget Jesus' prayer in the Garden of Gethsemane? He cried out that His soul was crushed with grief to the point of death. He was honest with His Father, wanting the awful hour to pass Him by, "Abba! Father! All things are possible for Thee; remove this cup from Me; yet not what I will, but what Thou wilt."[41]

Just as Jesus was transparent with His Father, we should call out to Him with our full range of emotions. Our Savior, who was without sin, experienced and voiced a vast variety of feelings, releasing them as they occurred. We see Him angry in the Temple, sad and shedding tears about the unbelief surrounding the death of Lazarus, and anguished in the Garden. At times He was filled with joy (Luke 10:21); at other times He showed astonishment and wonder (Mark 6:6, Luke 7:9). Sometimes He felt distress (Mark 3:5, Luke 12:50). But perhaps Jesus' greatest verbal expression of grief and anguish came during His last moments on the cross, "My God, My God, why hast Thou forsaken me?"[42]

The Holy Spirit Grieves

Not only did the Heavenly Father and God the Son grieve, but the Holy Spirit also grieved and did His grief work. We're told, ". . . do not grieve the Holy Spirit of God, by whom you were sealed for the day of redemption."[43] God doesn't need any tools to do His grief work, because His memory is immediate and complete. All that's ever happened is instantly and perfectly known to Him. And, of course, God doesn't need to apologize to us, because He makes no mistakes and does not sin.

The writer of Ecclesiastes understood that human beings needed to embrace the various seasons that are a part of life. There's ". . . a time to cry and a time to laugh. A time to grieve and a time to dance"[44] It's important to notice that the joy of dancing is fully *expected* to come *after* the work of grieving!

Paul taught the Thessalonians, "But we do not want you to be uninformed, brethren, about those who are asleep, that you may not grieve, as do the rest who have no hope."[45] Christians can rejoice in the hope of resurrection and eternal life.

Hope resides in the intuitive aspects of human personality. Our intuition provides instinctive, immediate knowledge that's available without the conscious use of reason. It's sometimes understood as "a knowing in one's heart." Most maturing believers have experienced memorable situations where God came through for us. These positive encounters form a principle of hope in our core beliefs. When difficult situations arise, we know without reasoning or thinking about it, that God is for us not against us. It's not that we don't hurt and struggle through grief, but we have a supernatural element of hope that's mixed with our hurt and struggle.

In order to have a deep relationship with us, God forgives us and washes us clean, and in order to encourage us and to reveal His loving nature, God makes significant emotional statements, and He keeps those current, through the Holy Spirit, His Word, and His people. God has already written His completion letter; it's a love letter, and it's called the Bible.

CHAPTER 7
MISINFORMATION AND
MYTHS ABOUT GRIEF

In the United States, we're taught how to acquire things, not what to do when we lose them. In addition, we aren't taught what to do about grief. We've received misinformation and myths about grief taught to us by our parents, pastors, teachers, or friends who learned from their parents, pastors, teachers, or friends. Therefore, we've been saddled with what was passed on to us, and we are passing it on to our children and others, purely from a lack of never being taught a better way. Here are six unhelpful concepts commonly perpetrated upon a griever:

1. Don't feel bad.

2. Replace the loss.

3. Grieve alone.

4. It just takes time.

5. Be strong for others.

6. Keep busy.[46]

As the authors of *The Grief Recovery Handbook* note, "None of these ideas leads us to the actions of discovering and completing the unfinished emotions that accrue in all relationships."[47] In addition to misinformation and myths about grief, we should ready ourselves for the fact that most people will be ill-prepared to help us deal with loss. They don't know what to say, so they say things that are insensitive. We honor the Lord, however, when we ask Him to help us forgive the people who have blindsided us with hurtful statements.

I Thought I Was A Good Christian

I'd been a Christian for fourteen years, participating in many wonderful Bible studies, going to church every time the doors opened (which back then was a minimum of three times a week), and studying at a Bible College to be a missionary when I met and married my first husband. I thought that I was a good Christian, an example to others of how God could restore a person back to wholeness after having been down the hapless road of the world. I never had a clue that something wasn't right until after I married my husband and lived with him twenty-four hours a day.

One evening my husband told me that the reason he married me was because he thought that I had something different--different from the other Christians he'd been around. But when he lived with me day in and day out, he'd discovered that I was just like everyone else. Was that ever a blow to me! Yet, in my heart, I knew he was right. This truth had totally escaped my radar screen. I'd thought I was doing well.

You see, no one had ever told me that we learn our ways of relating from our family. No one had explained the impact that unrighteous role models and acquired behaviors can have on you. No one had discussed how we coexist with the deep pains that lie buried within, or how we carry our past with us into our present, even after we've accepted Christ as our Savior.

Marriage takes more than love to work. I spent ten years of trying to make our relationship work, but neither of us had the relational skills we needed. In my family we were taught, "If you don't talk about it, it doesn't exist," and that confrontation brings abandonment, so communication wasn't valued in my growing up years. In fact, true communication was completely absent.

Needless to say, by the time I reached young adulthood, I was totally unable to express my feelings. I can't even imagine how frustrating it was to live with someone who never explained her needs. Even when a brief exchange escalated into an argument, I would turn into a silent, cold fish. Survival in my family meant not letting anyone know that you cared. So, I became an expert at disengaging. I could make my family feel just as "non-existent" as I felt. I suppose that was my way of retaliating at an unconscious level. Those were skills that helped me to survive as a child, but they didn't work very well in my adult relationships.

My marriage might have turned out differently if in my Christian discipleship process, I'd been taught the importance of addressing the past, so it didn't follow me around the rest of my life. The focus was on burying the past, and preachers and teachers just skipped right over my heart and filled my head with lots of knowledge "about" God and the Scriptures. Another focus was on "looking like a Christian," and working towards an outward appearance that fit into what the preacher deemed holy.

One time we had a revival, and I brought some inner city kids to the church, hoping they would have an opportunity to learn about Jesus and become believers. After the service, I was told not to bring them again. You see, these kids wore shorts, and unless they looked a certain way, they weren't welcome into our "proper" sanctuary to hear about Jesus. I've often wondered what happened to those girls. Where would most of us be if Jesus had required us to "clean up" before He would talk to us? So, if you're reading this, and you feel like your life's a literal mess or a farce that's well-dressed, don't despair. God has been looking at your heart the whole time; appearances mean nothing to Him. One of God's most beloved prophets ran around naked because God asked him to; others, like John the Baptist, were under a God-given vow never to cut their hair. Pray for truth, no matter what your circumstances look like, and watch what revelations come your way!

CHAPTER 8
IDENTIFYING SHORT-TERM
ENERGY RELIEVING BEHAVIORS

According to the authors of *The Grief Recovery Handbook*:

"The death of a loved one, divorce, and all other losses produce an incredible amount of emotional energy. Since we have all been socialized from early on to deal with sad, painful, and negative emotions incorrectly, we end up storing the energy inside ourselves.

"A caretaker may say, "Don't cry, here, have a cookie, you'll feel better," thus setting the child up with a lifetime belief, from an important authority source, that feelings can be fixed with food. (This was illustrated in one line from the *The Matrix*, when the Oracle offered Neo a cookie.)

"Upon eating the cookie, the child feels different, not better, and for the moment is distracted and forgets about the loss event. However, there has been no completion of the emotional pain caused by the event. The event and the feelings attached to it are now buried under the cookie, the sugar, and the distraction. So, early on, we learn to cover up, hide, or bury our feelings under food."[48]

Many of us have observed friends and family members consuming copious amounts of food and alcohol after a funeral or a divorce. "Food and alcohol are obvious and typical short-term-energy-relieving behaviors (STERBs). There are many other short-term behaviors that have the same life-limiting and damaging consequences."[49]

Here is a partial list of behaviors that can have a negative impact on grieving people:

- "Food
- Alcohol/Drugs
- Anger
- Exercise
- Fantasy (movies, TV, books)
- Isolation
- Sex
- Shopping (humorously called retail therapy)
- "Workaholism"

Most of these actions are not harmful in and of themselves, but they can become harmful when engaged in for the wrong reasons."[50]

Also, as Christians, we know that *anything* we turn to for comfort, before turning to God, has become an idol in our hearts. That's why taking stock of our habits and behaviors can help us to identify areas for which we need to repent.

Many Christians practice religion as a way to avoid processing grief. For example, Susan was already quite involved in her ministry to senior adults at her church when her husband was diagnosed with Huntington's disease. She didn't want to dwell on the implications this held for their long-term future. Her ministry provided an escape from her grief about the loss of her hopes, dreams, and expectations. She developed several methods to help people in her ministry group grow deeper in their relationship with God. She participated in efforts to bring an evangelistic program into her church, sang in the choir, and wrote devotionals and sermons. These were all worthwhile endeavors, "good works" for the Lord. However, by working on these projects, she consumed time and energy that she needed to process her grief.

The institutional church relies on the energy and enthusiasm of its members to function. It's ironic that the same institution which provides solace and opportunities to grow closer to God, also offers myriad ways to divert a griever's attention from completing the emotions associated with a loss. Religiosity takes workaholism a step deeper, because it is cloaked in the guise of spiritual worthiness. Religiosity also claims that Grief Recovery® tools are unnecessary if you "really believe." Grievers sometimes avoid the agonizing examination of their emotions with the assertion that God has already taken away their pain on the cross.

This pattern of working to please God becomes a STERB (a short-term energy relieving behavior) to decrease or hide the pain of loss. Thus many people seek God, not to have a relationship with Him, but to move around in His arena to relieve the pain in their lives. Even though this is very difficult for most people to see, this STERB can become as addictive and destructive as other STERBs. Religion *drives* people, but the love of Jesus Christ *draws* people.

Peter Scazzero describes this STERB as "using God to run from God." He offers some examples from his own experiences:

--When I do God's work to satisfy me, not Him.

--When I do things in His name He never asked me to do.

--When my prayers are really about God doing my will, not my surrendering to His.

--When I demonstrate "Christian behaviors" so significant people think well of me.

--When I focus on certain theological points ("Everything should be done in a fitting and orderly way" [1 Corinthians 14:40]) that are more about my own fears and unresolved issues than concern for God's truth.

--When I use His truth to judge and devalue others.

--When I pronounce, "The Lord told me I should do this" when the truth is, "I think the Lord told me to do this."

--When I use Scripture to justify the sinful parts of my family, culture, and nation instead of evaluating them under His Lordship.

--When I hide behind God talk, deflecting any spotlight on my inner cracks and becoming defensive about my failures.

--When I apply biblical truths selectively, when it suits my purposes, but avoid situations that would require me to make significant life changes."[51]

According to Scripture, works done in the flesh (not directed by God to you personally and thus not emanating from His heart to your heart) will burn up. So they're just a waste of our time and energy. They can become distractions from our real issues, giving us a false sense of security and well being. If they're not what is God asking for, they're foolish and disobedient activities. They might just be religious STERBs.

While many short-term relief behaviors are apparent, some, like religion, are not.

"It's not uncommon for people to visit gravesites on an extremely regular basis for years following a death. Unconsciously, these grievers are seeking some relief from pain caused by the incomplete relationship. The problem is that visiting the grave doesn't lead to permanent relief or completion with the person who died."[52]

Since we intellectually know that these behaviors don't work and can be destructive, why and how do we become trapped in them? The answer is in a Grief Recovery® truism: When your heart is broken, your head doesn't work right, and your spirit can't soar. The Bible says something very close to this in Isaiah: "Why do you continue to invite punishment? Must you rebel forever? Your head is injured, and your heart is sick."[53]

God was trying to help His people see that their rebellion only invited punishment. So why did they continue to rebel? He answers this question in the next sentence, "Your head is injured, and your heart is sick!" When your heart is broken, your head doesn't work right, and your spirit can't soar (because it's burdened, weighted down, imprisoned, or chained). You were created to have a spirit that soars with the eagles, but instead, you can be trapped in a barnyard of pecking chickens, looking down instead of up.

Three Major Problems with STERBs

Let's examine what can happen when our hearts are broken and incapable of releasing energy or feelings. *The Grief Recovery Handbook* uses the example of a steam kettle. A healthy steam kettle releases steam immediately as it builds up, and so should we. Now, think about a steam kettle heating up, but having a cork placed in the spout. This is dangerous, and eventually, there's going to be some kind of explosive relief. "The cork represents a lifetime of misinformation that causes us to believe that we are not supposed to talk about sad, painful, and negative emotions."[54] When our release is blocked, we may start participating in STERBs, which can create three major problems:

1. They work, or more accurately, they *appear* to work. They create an illusion of recovery by causing you to forget or bury your emotions, at least the more painful ones.
2. They are short-term. They do not last and they do nothing to deal with the emotional issue. This is why the STERB must be participated in over and over, and can become addictive.

3. They do nothing to remove the cork jammed in the spout. In fact, most people don't even realize there is a cork in the spout.[55]

The accumulation of unresolved grief issues will eventually lead to either over-reactive behavior or an explosion. Have you ever had an emotional reaction larger than the circumstances called for? Sadly, we all have to say, "Yes!" Bottling up our feelings will lead to such an explosion. The explosion may be in any one of the STERBs or another area. The explosion may be sexual infidelity or financial indiscretion or violent anger. Most of know about Winona Ryder's being convicted of vandalism and felony grand theft. We think, *Why would a superstar do something like that?* Superstars are people, just like you and me, who have unresolved grief issues that can explode! None of us are immune. The actions of Grief Recovery® will help us remove the cork.

<u>Physiological Impact of Stuffing Emotions</u>

Emotions can also be described as energy. According to the laws of physics, energy can't just disappear; it has to go somewhere. If the energy builds up and is not released, then it's internalized. This can take an enormous toll on one's physical health, resulting in many different diseases and disorders. Recall the illustration of the kettle; it takes an enormous amount of energy to keep that cork stuffed down in the spout. That's energy that our immune system needs for its daily functioning. Displacing this energy can cause our immune system to break down.

In the medical community, we've known about the mind/body connection for over twenty years.

However, the limitations of scientific research hampered our ability to produce "hard data" to prove it. Most often, we were left with only "soft data" to report the connection. It's an exciting time now in the field known as psychoneuroimmunology, because today we have a lot of new "hard data" to show how feelings can actually change the chemicals in our brain, resulting in cellular changes in our body tissues at the molecular level.

So what does this all mean? It supports the concept that stuffing down our feelings can take a physical toll on our bodies, and that destructive habits, coupled with genetic predispositions, can cause various illnesses to manifest. Our bodies are in a constant state of stress, which, of course, adds to their eventual breakdown. Examples of some of these illnesses are heart disease, strokes, migraines, gastrointestinal disorders, and cancer. Depression is another disorder seen in individuals who stuff their emotions.

Given this picture, it's easy to see why so many of us are walking time bombs. Holding in our emotions will negatively impact our relationships because of our over-reactive or explosive behavior. If we stuff down our feelings, that negative stored energy will attack our bodies (and minds). God did not design us to be storage tanks. He designed us as processing plants! We need to be responsible to ourselves and others, and allowing our emotions to be released as we experience them is one aspect of healthy living.

CHAPTER 9
WHAT IS THE GRIEF RECOVERY PROGRAM?

Since Grief Recovery® is not a spiritual discipline (not prayer, fasting, Bible reading) but an emotional program, it can be done by believers as well as non-believers. In addition, since the principles and actions are based on principles of truth which are in keeping with the Bible, they'll work, to some degree, with anyone who will do the actions.

Yet, as believers, we still need the Holy Spirit in conjunction with the use of this tool, to be as effective as possible. Why? Because Satan has a master plan to try to keep us deceived about the true nature of our hearts. If Satan can convince us that we don't harbor resentments, disappointments, distrust, or any other undelivered communication with God, then he's won the battle of keeping us disconnected from our energy source and our intimacy with God. For this reason, we need the Lord to test our hearts and to search our minds, through the Holy Spirit, to offset the lies of Satan.

The Holy Spirit, in revealing truth, encourages us, and provides the boldness and tenacity to do the necessary work. He's our Mighty Counselor and our Omniscient Teacher, the one who gives us hope and courage. Let me make one thing clear: I never advocate tools in place of the Holy Spirit. However, countless times I've witnessed how certain tools opened a door for the Holy Spirit to do His healing work, and I believe tools can often put us in a better position to receive His divine help.

Grief Recovery® is a specific set of action steps that give you a practical pathway to complete any unresolved emotions regardless of the loss event. Whether you're aware of unfinished business or you're not totally convinced you need help, your life can be radically changed for the better if you will press on and complete this work. The success rate for this program is incredibly high as long as you are willing to do two things. First, be willing to be honest about your emotional truth, and second, follow the steps, and do the work as it is outlined. There aren't any shortcuts!

Fear is a natural reaction when approaching the unknown and unfamiliar. Acknowledging the fear, and then taking the steps anyway, will lead to incredible gifts. If you ask the Holy Spirit, He will help you push through the tough spots.

This program is not a replacement for God's healing power. He's the only one who can heal completely. However, He has chosen to reveal these practical keys to us, so that our hearts can be cleared of all that separates us from Him.

Satan is the master deceiver, and if he can convince us that we're fine, then he will have won the battle, and we will never live up to the potential which God has called us. We must recapture that which the enemy has stolen--our hearts. When our hearts are closed because of distrust, fear, or pain, it results in separation from God's greatest love and power. With closed hearts, we'll never be able to love Him the way He wants us to, nor will we ever be able to experience the depth of His love and care for us as long as there is anything that prevents Him from inhabiting every inch of our hearts. Hearts begin to heal during Grief Recovery®. So what does recovery look like? Here's a practical picture:

- Recovery means feeling better.
- Recovery means claiming your circumstances instead of your circumstances claiming you and your happiness.
- Recovery is finding new meaning for living, without the fear of being hurt again.
- Recovery is being able to enjoy fond memories without having them precipitate painful feelings of regret or remorse.
- Recovery is acknowledging that it's perfectly all right to feel sad from time to time and to talk about those feelings no matter how those around you react.
- Recovery is being able to forgive others when they say or do things that you know are based on their lack of knowledge about grief.
- Recovery is one day realizing that your ability to talk about the loss you've experienced is indeed normal.
- Most importantly, recovery means acquiring the skills that we should have been taught in childhood. These skills allow us to deal with the loss directly.[56]

Unlike support groups, this program is designed to provide the participants with tools that will enable them to move beyond their losses to a richer quality of life. Grievers have never lacked the courage to recover. What they've lacked is the "how to" information. Many people whose faith has been damaged by an overwhelming loss, or by an accumulation of losses over a lifetime, have discovered that these actions free their spirit, help heal their hearts, and enhance their relationship with God and others.

A Grief Counselor's Goals

What I cannot describe on paper is God's anointing that allows me to accomplish His goals in a particular session, but what I can say is that I try to create a safe community that fosters awareness and transformation. When, in all transparency, I tell the truth about my past, I bequeath a gift of hope. It is what God requires of me, and it positions the group to receive the supernatural power that God has for them. Through the grace of the Holy Spirit, I am sensitive to the needs and concerns of the group. We all enjoy people who confess to being human, so I always model activities before having others engage in them.

Opening my heart to clients helps them feel engaged and more inspired to have an authentic experience of their own, where honesty and truth are central, and God's healing fire, His all-consuming, unconditional love can engulf the hearts of participants. By going inward, clients find God. When we seek Him in this way, He does not allow us to stay in a place of selective forgetting (denial), minimizing, blaming others, blaming ourselves, rationalizing, or intellectualizing.

Half of the activities we engage in involve some casual writing. There is a reason for this, and a reason that I share my personal stories: storytelling engages all the senses; it triggers activity on both the left and right sides of the brain. Because stories elicit whole brain and whole body responses, they almost always evoke strong emotions. I have heard it said that a true piece of writing is a dangerous thing because it can change your life. Each person's voice is like a snowflake—complicated, beautiful, and individual.

Our stories can shed light on our moral assignments: we can begin to see how God can use what we've been through for His Kingdom purposes if we let Him. The difference between happy and unhappy people is that happy people have found a use for themselves, like a good tool. Our culture's dysfunctional message is that healthy people accept the world as it is, but I refuse to call what is sick, healthy, and I refuse to believe lives can't be changed.

Grief Recovery® Actions

Before moving forward, I need to touch on some very important principles. I want to remind you again that we should never compare losses! Why? Everyone experiences pain at 100%. We've become so used to comparing losses that it may take a little time to fully appreciate this concept. Second, I want to remind you that you're the only one who can stop your recovery. It's in your hands. Third, this work is about reaching emotional truth. The events are less important than recognizing and telling the emotional truth. Truth is the Person of Jesus, and knowing Him sets us free. All we have to lose by doing this work is depression, pain, and sleepless nights.

The Past Is Closer Than It Appears

Some powerful people within the church may voice objections to revisiting the past. They might say, "What's in the past should stay in the past," or "We don't have to drudge up the past to get well." Because these people are so respected, we might believe that lie. Having worked with thousands of grievers, I say it's time to accept a healing truth.

Bishop Joey Johnson shared this experience with me. One evening God pointed out to him the words stenciled in white on his passenger's side rearview mirror: *"Objects in Mirror Are Closer Than They Appear."* The bishop had just begun a series called "The Ravages of Rejection." It revolved around the history of the nation of Israel. Moses had prophesied that rejection would continue to impact Israel in the future. The past was closer than it appeared, and anyone who keeps up with world politics can easily see that rejection is still affecting that nation's present.

Recall what Paul exhorted: "Brethren, I do not regard myself as having laid hold of it yet; but one thing I do: forgetting what lies behind and reaching forward to what lies ahead."[57] Let's remember, unresolved loss events and their pain aren't in the past, but in the present. Paul is talking about living fully in the present!

We're to *learn* from the past, *live* in the present, and *look towards* the future! So how do we live fully and freely in the present, if we've never been fully free of the pain of the past? The only way to move towards this goal is to complete the issues of the past. This is where Grief Recovery® can be extremely helpful.

- Grief Recovery® is a program with tools to help people recover from loss one heart at a time.
- Grief Recovery® is a program with tools that help believers do deep repentance.
- The Grief Recovery® program helps us contend with what lies behind us and reach toward what lies ahead of us by helping us to complete the incomplete loss issues that motivate us to STERBS and to sin!
- Grief Recovery® helps us understand that when we are incomplete with our past, we are likely to recreate it in the future.
- Grief Recovery® helps us see that when we are incomplete with our past, we will have no choice but to embrace fear.

CHAPTER 10
GRIEF RECOVERY ACTION STEP 1
THE LOSS HISTORY GRAPH

Before I explain the specific action steps, remember that Grief Recovery® is not a magic formula. It's a tool that can be used to help you recover from loss, complete incomplete relationships, and become aware of emotional truth. We, on the staff of The Grief Recovery Institute, believe that all losses and pain happen in the context of relationships. I've heard Russell Friedman, my mentor and co-author of *The Grief Recovery Handbook,* say so many times that, "People have a relationship to their pain or addiction status and they get stuck.

There comes a point when they, because of their familiarity with their pain, dig in their heels." Immediately, the fear of the unknown kicks in. "Who will I be without my pain?" they wonder. And sadly, some people won't choose to complete the pain in their relationships because it meets a need for them. Yet, for all the thousands of people we've seen who pressed in, we've seen the huge majority walk out in freedom.

Grief Recovery® is a tool that can help you get unstuck, but the absolute best way to recover from an overwhelming loss or an accumulation of losses is to do deep repentance by inviting Jesus into the secret places in your heart. Steve Chapman's song "The Secret Place" beautifully reveals how Jesus can bring His healing light to touch our darkest memories.

The Secret Place

My Heart is like a house; one day I let the Savior in. There were many rooms, where we would visit now and then. But then one day He saw the door, I knew that day had come too soon. I said, "Jesus, I'm not ready, for us to visit in that room. That's a place in my heart, where even I don't go. I have some things hidden there; I don't want anyone to know." But He handed me the keys, with tears of love on His face. He said, "I want to make you clean; let Me go in your secret place." So I opened up the door, and as the two of us walked in I was so ashamed; His light revealed my hidden sin (pain). But when I think about that room now, I'm not afraid anymore, 'Cause I know my hidden sin (pain), no longer hides behind that   door.

It was the place in my heart, where even I wouldn't go. I had some things hidden there I didn't want anyone to know. But he handed me the keys, with tears of love on His face. He made me clean. I let Him in my secret place.[58]

Action Step #1: The Loss History Graph

The Loss History Graph is designed to help you discover what losses have occurred in your life and which of them are restricting your day-to-day living. It might seem strange for you to hear that you need to identify the losses in your life. After all, shouldn't you know what they are? Sadly, most people aren't aware of the emotions from past events that still hinder their lives. The goal of this graph is to make us aware of our losses, so that we can discover what misinformation we were taught directly or absorbed from our culture.

We start this graph with your first conscious memory. That memory, in and of itself, may not seem particularly compelling, but that's all right; we're interested in beginning the process of recalling memories, and somehow starting with that first memory seems to begin the unlocking of closed or hidden doors to rooms that have long been shut.

In order for others to have the courage to do their work, the facilitator always goes first, modeling the behavior for the group or individual. This is a powerful part of the program because we're modeling how to be real, open, and honest.

I'm including my Loss History Graph because the Lord has required this transparency from me, and I'm happy to do whatever He asks if it will help others reach and resolve the hindering parts of their lives. I also include this graph because it conveys God's greatness, His healing power that mended my broken heart and helped me resolve decades of painful situations and relationships.

As you read you may be flooded with your own memories; that's good. Keep a pad by your side, and dash down whatever memories or thoughts come to mind. Later on, you can figure out the years when these events occurred. My Loss History Graph has been expanded here to reveal a number of emotional losses and to convey a lifetime of pain and disappointment. Its detail and length reveal God's unfailing faithfulness to turn darkness into treasure.

When I lead Grief Recovery groups and trainings, I condense this graph to a thirty-minute demonstration. Participants are encouraged to write a Lost History Graph with significant emotional events listed on the graph. They share this information with their partner in a thirty-minute time frame.

Nancy Stutz-Martin's Loss History Graph:

1954: My First Conscious Memory

My first conscious memory occurred when I was four years old. Our family owned a black cocker spaniel named George. He was a frisky dog, and sometimes when we went to visit my grandmother, we would bring George. My aunt lived with my grandmother, and we would play with her children, my cousins.

One afternoon George began chasing Bobby, my cousin who was about six at the time. Bobby squealed in fright which definitely added an element of zeal to George's pursuit. Bobby wore pants with an elastic waistband. George ran behind Bobby, snapping hold of his pants and pulling. Eventually, George toppled Bobby, and once they were both on the ground, the dog was able to pull Bobby's pants all the way down. The rest of us laughed so hard our sides hurt.

We thought it was the funniest thing. That dog sure had it out for Bobby for some reason. In retrospect, I think it's obvious that some adult should've come to Bobby's rescue and told us not to laugh at another person's fear.

1959: My Parents Divorce

Before I describe the circumstances regarding the divorce, I need to paint a picture of what my childhood was like, giving some details of our less-than-perfect home life. In 1948, my parents married at the age of eighteen. My mom was a senior in high school and started writing to my dad while he was overseas in the Marines. He came home on leave, and my mom quit school two months before graduation to marry him. I think she just wanted out of her home.

In 1950, two years later, my mom had two appointments in one day, the first with the doctor and the second with an attorney to file for divorce. Dr. Jolly informed her that she was pregnant. She began to cry and told him her plans. He told her that she was going back home to her husband, and he picked up the phone and called my dad to come pick her up.

We lived in Chattanooga until I was a little over one. Then we moved to Camp Pendleton, California. My middle sister was born there, thirteen days before my second birthday. My mom had toxemia and almost died with her. I believe that's why they had such an incredible bond. They always looked alike.

When I was five, we moved to Camp Le Jeune, North Carolina, where my youngest sister was born a year later. Life was very strange in our house. My dad was gone all the time. I remember thinking, *Why do all the other dads come out and play with their children and my father never does?*

When Dad wasn't gone, however, he had a ritual. Upon returning home at the end of a day, he'd walk over to the TV, empty the change from his pockets into a crystal dish that sat on top of it, and lie down on the sofa to take a nap. When he awoke, my mom would have dinner ready. And after she cleaned the kitchen, she would go run his bath water, and lay his next day's clothes out on the bed for him. Our house was run like the Marine Corp. I remember my dad making me sing the

Marine Corp anthem, but I don't recall ever having any one-on-one time with him.

My mother told me the following story, but I have no memory of it. Apparently, when I was five, I informed her that I was going to run away. Her reply was, "Well, let me fix you some food, so you don't get hungry on your trip." Mom made me a sandwich, tied it up in a little handkerchief, and then kissed me good-bye and sent me out the door. I proceeded to walk down to the end of the corner, and then, not knowing what to do, I sat down on the curb. (Mom was watching me from the window the whole time.) When it started to get dark, she said I walked back to the house, knocked on the door, and asked if I could come home now. Something in my spirit wasn't happy with the way things were at home, but I never tried to run away again. Mom cured me of that.

That same year I was kicked out of kindergarten. The teacher had told us to go up to the row of easels to paint. I couldn't find an easel, that wasn't already taken, so I didn't know what to do. And because I'd never learned to communicate, I didn't understand that I should've gone back to tell the teacher that I couldn't find a place to paint. So I stood there, and then she yelled at me to get in place, so I hurried over and started painting on the other side of someone else's easel on the side where the paper had been flipped over. Well, the teacher became livid and kicked me out of her class, and I had to go to a different class. Have you ever met anyone who got kicked out of kindergarten?

In searching for memories, I was thrilled when, finally, a good one came to mind. In the summer of

1955, we had a black Pontiac. Dad took us to get ice cream, and he let me sit in his lap and steer. My sister and I would tell him to go faster, and he would. Then, suddenly, he'd put on the brakes, and we'd jerk forward and laugh. I don't remember any other time ever laughing with my dad; this was a rare occasion.

In 1956, when I was six, my mom left my dad. She put us on a bus, and we went to my grandparents' house in Chattanooga. She apparently started dating a disc jockey at a local radio station. When she discovered she was pregnant, she high-tailed it back to North Carolina. When my dad found out she was pregnant, he never believed the baby was his. The arguing and fights escalated. One night we were all at a friend's house and Mom and Dad broke into an argument. He took the car and left. My mom and the two of us girls had to walk a long way home. When we arrived, he grabbed my mom and took her into the bedroom and began hitting her.

When I was nine, my parents divorced. One day we lived in Camp Le Jeune, and the next day we were living in Chattanooga. There was a mantra in my family: "If you don't talk about it, it doesn't exist," so we never did talk about things. About a year and a half later, I saw my mom getting in the car with a man I hadn't seen before. I asked my grandmother why Mom was with that man, and she answered, "Your mom has a date." "What about my dad?" I asked. She looked at me bewildered. "Nancy, don't you know they got a divorce?" Nobody ever told me, and I didn't understand to ask.

Loss In Moving: Twelve Schools in Twelve Years

Starting in the first grade, I went to twelve schools in twelve years. We moved because my dad was in the military, but after the divorce, my mom continued the habit. Any time things were not going well, she would pick up and start all over again, believing that this time it would be better. I had to constantly lose and make friends.

1962: My Grandmother Dies

After my parents divorced, my grandmother came to live with us. Mom worked second shift, and Grandmother cared for us while she was gone. At twenty-nine Mom was single with three small children. She had neither parenting skills nor a high school education, and she was too busy trying to survive to truly be a mom.

My grandmother was the only person that I received nurturing from during the three years she lived with us. She was the person who introduced me to church. She'd take me with her when she could get a ride there. One thing you knew about my grandmother is that she loved God. There was never any question about that. She'd often have the preacher over for Sunday dinner. As long as my grandmother lived, she cooked chicken, mashed potatoes, green beans, biscuits, and gravy for Sunday dinner.

If Grandmother wasn't feeling well, I'd walk the six blocks to East Lake Baptist Church. The summer before my tenth birthday, I was sitting in the third row, listening to the preacher, when it hit me. At that moment, I realized that I was a sinner, and that God wanted me! He really wanted me! The musicians began to play, "Just As I Am," and I was out of my seat like lightning. At the altar I realized I'd been searching for someone who loved me, and I'd found Him while sitting on that tear-stained bench. From that moment on, I never again felt alone. I'd be at church Sunday morning, Wednesday night, and any other time the doors were open. It was my sanctuary.

About a week or so after my conversion, the pastor came to see my mom. My bike was lying on the sidewalk, and he had to step over it to reach the front door. That embarrassed me for some reason. The pastor asked my mother if it would be all right to baptize me. She gave her permission, and it was planned for the next Sunday night, August 20th, 1960. I wore a beautiful white robe. It was a powerful moment for me.

None of my family came that night to see me looking like an angel. But then, I didn't expect them to. They never took an interest in anything I did.

Grandmother, however, was proud of her little granddaughter, for choosing to give her life to Christ. My favorite memory is of her standing in church singing "Amazing Grace." Even today, that song often brings tears of joy to my eyes because that's such a precious memory for me. Our connection was that we both loved God. Grandmother wasn't perfect. She taught me how to cook, but also taught me and my cousin Ruth that sex was dirty and nasty. We believed her, and this caused us both many issues in our adult lives as we tried to overcome that lie. When grandmother couldn't go to church, she would let me walk down to East Lake Baptist Church. It became my sanctuary.

During the time my grandmother lived with us, my mom began dating a lawyer in town. He had given her an early Christmas present, a black negligee. My mom made the mistake of showing it to my grandmother. That started a huge argument, resulting in Grandmother's having a heart attack and my mom calling an ambulance. She died three days after my twelfth birthday, which was also three days after Christmas.

1962: First Safety Issue

My mom was the perfect example of that country western song "Looking for Love in All the Wrong Places." If there were ten men in a room and nine were perfect, my mom was like a magnet to that one bum. I remember as a child wanting to shake her and say, "Can't you see what you are doing?" It seemed very clear to me.

In 1962, a few months after breaking up with the lawyer who'd given her the negligee, Mom began dating this guy named David who had a son a year older than me. I was twelve and he was thirteen. On Friday nights, David would take the two of us roller skating. There used to be a rink at the corner of Brainerd Road and Germantown Road. It was a lot of fun. I was a good skater and enjoyed it very much. David taught me how to dance on skates.

After skating he'd drop off his son, and then, by the time we got back to my house, it was time for my mom to get home from her second-shift job.

Things were fine until one night he decided that he would take me parking up on Missionary Ridge in a secluded area of the park. I managed to escape with only his kissing me, but even that was pretty gross since I was twelve. That was an example of God's intervention. He gave me the wisdom to talk my way out of that situation.

I also knew that if I told Mom, she'd say it was my fault. So, I never told anyone, and just changed my life around as much as I had control over, so I would never have to go skating with him again. I made sure David and I were never left alone. One day a few weeks later, we were sitting at the kitchen table. David was helping me with my homework, and Mom, who'd been in the room with us, walked out for a moment to get something. While she was gone, he leaned over and kissed me. At that moment, Mom walked in through the back door and saw it. Now she was forced to give up the man she loved because of me. She blamed me, and somehow believed it was my fault.

Mom's Nervous Breakdown

Mom had always had her mother to fall back on, but now she was left alone at thirty-two with three kids. She had no one left, and the pressure of taking care of three children all alone was more than she could bear. Guilt and fear consumed her, and she had a nervous breakdown. I had to call the ambulance, and they came and took her off to Memorial Hospital. Here I was, twelve years old, and my mom was totally "out to lunch," leaving me to take care of my two younger sisters who were ten and six. I cooked, cleaned, and helped them with their homework. I walked them to school each day for three weeks until Mom was released from the hospital.

One night I asked my uncle to take me to the hospital to see her. He drove me there and waited in the car. When I returned, he was passed out drunk in the back seat, and no matter how I tried, I couldn't wake him up. So I had to drive the car home myself. I'd never driven before, but somehow God again gave me the ability and wisdom I needed, and I drove straight to our rental house. Thank goodness the car had an automatic transmission!

We Move to Atlanta

When Mom came back, she decided that she needed a change in scenery, so she moved alone to Atlanta. Mom's philosophy was that if things got bad, you move and start over. She thought new places made things better. The only flaw in her theory was that she hadn't figured out how not to bring her problems with her.

Before Mom left, she hired a lady to stay with us during the week. Once she found a job in Atlanta and a place to stay, she took my two sisters and put them in an orphanage until she could get on her feet again. I stayed in Chattanooga, moving into my aunt's house, so that I could finish the seventh grade. Then, when school was out, Mom moved into a larger apartment, took my sisters out of the orphanage, and had me to come and join them.

A couple of months later, I began the eighth grade. One day my mom went to the doctor because she wasn't feeling well. He told her to go home and stay in bed until he called her with the results of her blood test.

That afternoon he called and told her that she had a blood clot somewhere in her body and that she needed to call an ambulance right away and get to the hospital. Mom told him she couldn't do that because she had to make arrangements for her children, since we had no relatives living in the area. The doctor told her to stay in bed and not move around, warning her that she needed to get to the hospital as soon as possible.

Later that night Mom was standing in the kitchen, talking to my father on the phone, trying to tell him what was going on. She asked him if he could take us until she was released from the hospital. He said no, and as they were arguing, she fell unconscious to the floor.

I called an ambulance, and they took her to Crawford Long Hospital. We knew absolutely no one and were in a big city I wasn't familiar with. Mom was in a coma.

The next day, and the days to follow, I would get my sisters dressed, put them on their school bus, and then take my own bus to school. I went to O'Keefe High School (it started in 8th grade) which was in the middle of the Georgia Tech dorms. After school I walked a mile and a half to the hospital to check on my mom as she lay there in a coma. It was at least a six-mile walk home in the dark and took almost three hours. God had to be in the middle of all that because I have no idea how I found my way home each evening. Then I would feed my sisters, help them with homework, and get them off to bed.

I remember the afternoon I pleaded with Mom to wake up, and her eyes opened. I don't even have words to express the gratitude and relief I felt. Her coma had lasted seven days.

Some months later, Mom began dating an Air Force Recruiter named Steve Sergeant. He was a very nice man, and we liked him a lot. His wife was in a mental institution in Alabama. Back then the law wouldn't let him divorce her; at least that was my understanding as to why Mom and he didn't get married. They dated for almost a year.

Abruptly, one afternoon, Mom announced that we were to move back to Chattanooga over the weekend. But the very next morning, she woke us up early and told us to start packing, that my cousins were on their way over to help us move. I didn't have a chance to say good-bye to my friends or tell my employer at the movie theater that I wouldn't be back.

What Mom didn't want us to know is that she was pregnant with Steve Sergeant's baby. Back then, being divorced was a stigma enough, but being unwed and pregnant as well?! Mom, we learned many years later, was so embarrassed about her condition that she was determined to hide it from us at all costs. She was afraid if she told us that we wouldn't have any respect for her. Besides, she could barely feed us, so how was she going to take care of another child?

I was fourteen at the time. We hopped into the car and left Atlanta for my grandmother's old house back in Chattanooga. My aunt and her four children had been living there most of their lives. Since my grandmother had died, the house now belonged to my aunt and my mom. There were now seven children and two adults living in a two-bedroom house. My mom had the idea that she'd build an apartment on the back of the house, but that never came to pass.

I went to Chattanooga (City) High School in tenth grade and was on the drill squad. During our first game of the season, my mom came and watched me perform. That was the one and only time she ever came to anything I did. At the end of the summer, my mom put us into the Children's Home. She told us that she was having heart problems again and was going to Vanderbilt Hospital to be in a research study.

Given what had happened to her while we were in Atlanta, it made sense to me. Why would I have ever thought to doubt her? My mom gave the Children's Home my dad's child support check to help with our care. And we assumed she moved to Nashville. But she didn't. All that time she was living right near us in Chattanooga, at the Florence Crittington Home for unwed mothers.

Every once in a while, Mom would call and talk to us. Well, Christmas came, and my boyfriend's parents offered to drive me to Nashville to visit my mom. But she said oh no, that wasn't possible because the doctors thought it'd be too stressful for her to have visitors. Mom gave birth to a boy, and I believe he was born on February 22, 1965. One day I hope to find him and tell him the history of his "lost" family. I have a picture of Steve Sergeant, so if I ever find my brother, I will give it to him.

I want to take a moment to mention that living in the Children's Home was a wonderful reprieve for me. Since the facility usually only took children up till the age of twelve, I, at fourteen, was the oldest and given special privileges. I had my own bedroom and bathroom down a hallway away from the other children.

The housemother, Ruby, and I would drive together in her car to church, while the other children rode in a bus. Best of all, these were months of security, knowing I would be given three satisfying meals a day, and that I didn't have to be the caregiver of my younger sisters.

During this time, I felt a sense of freedom. The chores that were required, keeping my room and bathroom clean, were minimal compared to the onslaught of responsibilities to which I was accustomed.

1967: Second Safety Issue

After Mom gave up her baby boy for adoption, she moved to Miami to start over. We stayed in the Children's Home until I finished the tenth grade. When the school term ended, Ruby put the three of us on a Greyhound bus, and we went to Florida to live with her.

A year or so later, Mom began dating Bill, who was, in my opinion, a bum. Bill was an only child and was used to being the center of attention. He had to be right on every subject. We learned very early on just to agree with everything he said. It just made life easier that way. One night Mom, my sisters, and Bill were sitting at the dinner table, and he started on one of his theatrical performances.

Well, something rose up in me. I was seventeen, and I had one of those moments when I was fed up with everything, and I couldn't resist disagreeing with what he said. To this day I don't remember the subject, but in my opinion he never talked about anything important. Bill jumped up from his seat (he could have won a Golden Globe award for his dramatic episodes) and picked up a knife from the table and threw it at me. I could feel the wind as it sailed by my ear and landed in the wall. I know that he never intended to hurt me. He wasn't a violent person, but in his performance he'd gotten carried away. The result, however, was a turning point in my life. My mom stood up from the table and said, "I will not give up another man for you. You can pack your bags and get the hell out of my house!"

The next day I went to look for an apartment. I had a job at Mercy Hospital working in the lab, so I could pay the rent. I found a one-room apartment, rented it, and moved in. My mother's words had hurt me, but I could take care of myself. The money I'd been earning I could now spend on me instead of my family. It didn't crush me that I wasn't living with her, but it was sad that this situation was typical of her kind of choices. After that night Mom and I talked to each other every once in a while, but we had never had a close relationship anyway. It was more of a casual thing, and we never spoke about the incident after I moved out.

God clearly had His hand on me during my teenage years. I believed that if I worked hard, I could take care of myself, and not have to rely on others, who, from my viewpoint, were always unreliable. From the age of fourteen, I worked to help support the family, which meant that I had to be at the hospital by 3 p.m. where I worked until 11 p.m. So between 11 p.m. and 5:30 a.m., I had to get home, do my homework, and sleep. The amazing thing was I earned good grades, but I didn't really have time to study: I know that God supernaturally helped me pass my tests!

<u>1969: Abandonment Issue: New York City</u>

It was during the summer after my first year of college that I met a girl named Maria from Queens.

We were working together at a restaurant in Miami Beach. We heard that there was going to be a pop festival in Atlanta, so we took my car and headed to Atlanta. It was a Volkswagen and the starter was broken, so we had to push it to get it to start. Anyway, at the festival they announced that Woodstock would be in August in New York. So Maria talked me into moving to New York, so we could go to Woodstock. She said I could stay with her at her parent's home. She had a boyfriend named Jeff whom she talked into going as well. None of us had any money, but I had a car. So the three of us piled into the car and took off for New York. Gas only cost twenty-seven cents a gallon back then.

We arrived in Manhattan around one a.m. Maria said that she couldn't go to her mom's that late, so we were going to have to find a place to stay. I'd never been to New York before. Maria found us a cheap hotel down below 42nd Street in a very bad neighborhood. The place was a dump, occupied mostly by prostitutes. Maria and her boyfriend slept on the bed, and I stayed up all night, sitting in the chair with my feet propped up. There were roaches crawling everywhere. I'd never experienced anything like that before. I just waited for morning to arrive, so we could escape from there.

The next day we drove to her apartment building. Maria got out of the car and said, "See you!" She left us both sitting there, completely stunned. Her boyfriend was from California, and like me, this was his first time in New York. We sat in the car thinking, *What the heck are we going to do now?* My so-called friend had just used me for a ride to New York. We couldn't get into the building to go after her because we didn't know the apartment number to buzz us in.

So Jeff and I drove back into the city to find a hotel. We found one around 42nd Street that wasn't as bad as the other place. We parked the car. Between us we had about ten dollars. There was no choice but to sleep in the same bed. He didn't bother me. We were both exhausted and in a bad place.

The next morning we dressed and went off to find jobs. We planned to meet back at noon because that was the time my parking meter ran out. I took a bus to an employment agency. They sent me on an interview with an oil corporation on the 33rd floor of Rockefeller Center. I returned with a job.

Jeff had decided to try the subway. Well, he couldn't figure out how to get through the turnstiles, so he struck up a conversation with the man selling the tokens and told him about our dilemma. The guy said that he had an extra bedroom in his apartment. It was small and there had been a fire there once, but at least we would have a place to sleep. They lived in a basement apartment around 206th Street. This man was a bohemian guy with a Ph.D. who decided he didn't want to deal with the establishment, so instead just sold tokens in the subway. His wife also had a Ph.D. She was a concentration camp survivor. They were so nice to us.

The room they offered us was very small, full of boxes, and had not been painted since the fire. Worse, there was only one twin bed, and no room to sleep on the floor! The two of us had to make do with the twin bed, and while I was thankful Jeff didn't take advantage of the situation, all I could think was, *I've got to get out of here!*

My employer understood my need of an apartment, so after working four days that week, I was given a check, so I could begin looking for one. The next week I was in Macy's, riding the escalator. I had long hair down to my waist, and it was tied back with a big scarf. A couple of guys pulled at my scarf, and I turned around. They started a conversation, and I told them I was looking for an apartment.

One guy told me his friend's mother had an apartment for rent in Manhattan Beach. It was an apartment in the basement of her home, and she had rented it out to a lady for ten years, but the lady had recently died. It was in a safe neighborhood, so I agreed, and they took me over there. I spoke with his friend's mother, and she rented me the apartment. So that's how I escaped that situation.

I had some exciting times in New York City. I walked next to Shirley McLaine during a peace rally that ended at Madison Square Garden. Jimmy Hendrix came out around two in the morning. He staggered through one song and then collapsed. He had to be carried off stage.

You're probably wondering if I ever saw Maria again, my so-called friend who'd duped me. The answer is yes; I saw her one more time. Dumb me, I called her. She invited me to a party, and I went.

When I walked in, I could see everyone was sitting around getting high. This one guy said, "Do you want to make some A?" I had no idea what he was talking about, but I didn't want to appear to be a hick, so I said sure. He started putting this crystal stuff in a piece of tissue. He asked if that was enough, and I said, "No, I'll take a little more." Anyway, it turns out it was pure crystal amphetamine.

It was a wonder that I didn't die that night. My heart was about to beat out of my chest. I started jerking, and they couldn't get me to stop. It really scared them. Somehow they got me out of their apartment and back to Maria's. At that point the right side of my face went numb. Maria called a cab, and he took us to the hospital. The cab driver knew something was up, and he questioned us. Maria wouldn't answer and just kept saying, "Get us to the hospital!"

In the ER they gave me some meds and had me breathe into a paper bag. We were really scared that we were going to get busted and put in jail, so as soon as I felt like I could walk, we snuck out the side door. An ambulance driver saw us and followed us out. He asked what we were doing since I could barely walk. He felt sorry for us and offered to take us home. We were so paranoid that we had him drop us off around the block, so he wouldn't know where we were going if he decided to call the police. After he was gone, Maria tried to lead me around the block to her friend's apartment. I couldn't stand up and kept falling. It was a very long block.

Eventually, the drugs wore off, and I went home. That was the end of my relationship with Maria. By the grace of God, I survived that experience. I weighed only a hundred pounds and had taken enough crystal amphetamine to kill a man twice my size.

Soon after that, I heard about a great job that required a lot less typing than I was doing as a statistical typist for the oil company. There were little things I'd miss if I left the job, like riding up in the elevator each morning with Johnny Carson whose office was also in Rockefeller Center. Our conversation consisted solely of platitudes, "How are you?" and that kind of thing because I wasn't a communicator back then.

The new job I applied for was to be an assistant to the training manager of American Express. I'd be part of a team that made films all over New York State. During my first week I had a role as a stewardess and got to wear an official uniform. After a month or so, my boss called me into his office. Personnel had sent up my application with red circles on it. I was nineteen, but I'd changed my birth date to show that I was twenty-one.

My boss was disappointed, not because of the lie, but because we worked so well together, and he didn't want to fire me. But fire me he did; there was no way of getting around Personnel's red flag.

1970: Loss of Safety, Hawaii

It was November, and I didn't particularly care for cold weather, so I figured I'd fly down to Miami and visit Mom for the holidays. While there, she mentioned that her friend Mildred was living temporarily in Hawaii. Hawaii had been one of those exotic places I'd always wanted to visit. Mom said if I wanted to go, I had to leave ASAP because Mildred was due back in a few weeks. So I bought a plane ticket and left the following day. I had only fifteen dollars in my pocket, but that was enough because I'd stay with Mildred in Waikiki.

I applied for unemployment because of my being fired, and the fifty-five dollars I received each week was more than enough to support my bumming around. Since I barely ate anything (I was a vegetarian), and I barely wore more than my bathing suit, I didn't really have many expenses, so I moved out from Mildred and ended up renting a room in a bungalow on the beach. That gave me more freedom.

I loved Hawaii and planned to make it my home. But before my unemployment money ran out, I decided that I should take off for Europe first and then return to settle down in Hawaii. My friends had planned a going away party for me. On my way to the party, I walked down a side street that was not very well lit. An Asian man stuck a knife in my back and forced me into his parked car. He locked the doors and started the car with the knife at my throat. He told me if I tried anything, he'd kill me. He drove over to the other side of the island and back up into an isolated area that was mostly cane fields. He stopped the car at an obviously familiar place for him. He pulled me out of the car and threw me inside a tent.

Apparently, I wasn't the first person who'd been there because the blanket that covered the ground inside was covered in blood. He pulled my shorts off and crawled on top of me, proceeding to rape me as he held the knife at my throat. I remember closing my eyes and silently calling out to God. I just kept repeating Jesus over and over again until I blacked out.

The next thing I remember was waking up and realizing the nightmare was over. I surveyed the situation and realized that I had several options. I could put up a fight and then I would either be killed or left mangled for the rest of my life. Death was acceptable in my mind, but the thought of being left mangled was not. At that point an idea was dropped right into my head. Divine intervention. I could outsmart him by building his trust and waiting for the opportunity when he let his guard down. That is what I proceeded to do.

The guy said he was involved in the underworld, and that they were going to be sending him to France to take care of some business. So I told him I'd love to go with him. I spent the next several days building trust, getting him to talk about himself and acting like I cared.

The first day we left the tent, we drove to an area that was isolated except for a small country store. We went in to buy food. There was one old lady running the place, and no one else was around. Where could I run? It wasn't safe yet. On the way back to the tent, we passed some men working in the cane fields. I could've jumped out of the car at that point, but what would I be jumping into? The possibility of a mass rape? It wasn't yet safe.

We returned to the tent, and by the next day, he really trusted me. He said he needed to go pick something up at his boss's house. I acted very calm, so he didn't suspect anything. Earlier that morning I'd told him I was pregnant. We pulled up in his boss's driveway, and he went up to the door to pick up his package, watching me the entire time. When he returned to the car, I was huddled over, crying and jerking. He asked what was wrong. I was crying and screaming like I was scared to death and in horrific pain. I cried, "I'm losing the baby!" He didn't know what to do; it caught him so off guard. "I've got to get to the hospital to save the baby. Please help me!" I pleaded, in obvious distress.

Stunned, the guy drove me to the hospital which was only a few blocks away. I promised him that I'd be good and not say a word, that I wanted to go to France with him. He was helping to hold me up as we walked down the sidewalk to the ER. I could see as we got closer that he was beginning to have second thoughts, so I acted like I was passing out, and he had to pick me up just as one of the employees came running out to help. He stayed right by my side and would not leave.

The nurse helped lift me onto a bed. I had my arm around her neck and whispered, "Call the police." Fortunately, she figured something was up, so she told the man to wait in the chair across from the bed because she needed to get my clothes off. He did not want to cooperate, but she insisted. She told him, "You'll be in full view of the bed." Once she got him in the chair, she pulled the curtain around the bed. She leaned over, and I whispered, "He raped me. Please call the police. Please help me--he has a knife." The nurse helped me into a gown and told him she was going to fetch something for pain.

The chair he was sitting in was facing me, and his back was to the doorway. It was not long before two policemen walked up behind him and grabbed him. They put him in handcuffs and took him off to jail. The nurse came back in the room and held me as I cried, knowing I was finally safe. The detective came and talked with me. I was examined, and they took samples to confirm the rape. They also wanted my clothes. A detective took me to my apartment and let me change clothes. He took mine as evidence.

I had other situations in my life where I'd get myself into all kinds of messes. No matter what happened, God was always faithful and gave me a way of escape. When I look back on my life, I see that God didn't prevent the bad things from happening, but He was always there to help me. I knew in my deepest being that He was always with me, giving me directions if I would listen.

Meanwhile, my friends had been trying to figure out what was going on, why I'd never showed up for my party, and why I was giving my clothes to some man at the door. After the detective drove off, I began to cry and shared what had happened.

The detective had told me to come to the police station to press charges the next day, so they could begin court proceedings. I promised that I would be there, but as I began thinking about how rape cases were prosecuted (especially in the '70s), I knew that it would be easy for them to look at my lifestyle (a free-spirited, young woman who wasn't working and smoked pot) and use that against me. I would have endured the trial to keep that from happening to someone else, but the closer the time came, the more I felt strongly that it would be a waste of time and the man would go free, and my life would be exploited for nothing.

Instead, I boarded a plane the next day and left. My friend, Luanne, had left Hawaii to go to Medical Technology School in Berkeley. When I called her, she told me to get on a plane as fast as I could, that she would pick me up at the airport.

1970: Disillusionment with the Establishment, Mexico/Europe

Knowing that it was unlikely that I would receive justice in a rape trial, I decided to escape further into a life free of responsibilities. My friend Paul was just getting out of the Navy after his assignment in Hawaii, so he volunteered to go with me on my journey until I met some other people to travel with. After what had just happened in Hawaii, he didn't want me to be alone. He was a big husky guy, so he knew people wouldn't try to mess with me when he was around.

From Berkeley we made our way down to Los Angeles. In L.A. we decided to hop a freight train. In the train yard we saw a group of hobos. Paul wanted to lift me into a box car as soon as possible before those men saw me. So we climbed into an empty car and hid over in a corner, hoping no one else would crawl in after us. Thankfully, no one did, and the train pulled out.

It was beautiful, traveling with the door open and being able to see snow on the mountaintops in the middle of the desert. I had a wooden flute that a friend on the Big Island had made for me out of cane. I tried to play it, and we would dance around. When it got dark, we huddled in the corner again, trying to stay warm. The next day around noon, the train pulled into Tucson. As it slowed down, we jumped off with our backpacks and sleeping bags. Standing in the sunlight, I could see we were completely covered from head to toe in dirt.

We immediately went to find a laundromat and proceeded to wash all our clothes and sponge bathe in the bathroom. Paul made friends with some guy, and he took us to his house where we spent the night. The next day we began our adventure to Mexico, hitching a ride from Tucson to Nogales, where we crossed the border into Mexico.

It became apparent that we would not be very successful hitching a ride in this part of the country. We discovered that the first 1500 miles was mostly desert, so we took a train to Matalan. We stayed there, found some mescaline, and enjoyed the beautiful beach. Next, we were off to Mexico City by way of Guadalajara.

We were terrified that the police would stop us, throw us in jail, and we would rot there, and no one would ever know. So we were very careful. We hitched a ride with two guys in a big truck almost the size of an eighteen wheeler. The truck had a canvas roof, and the guys told Paul he could ride on top. They told me to get in the cab. So I was sitting between them as we drove along, and suddenly, I began to feel very uncomfortable, like this was not a good idea. I didn't know what to do or how to get out of the truck. Paul, apparently, was feeling uneasy as well, so he beat on the window of the cab for the guys to stop and let us off. I know that was another divine intervention!

Once in Mexico City we went to the University where Paul hooked up with a Mexican student who spoke English. His father was a doctor, and they had a big home, so he took us to his house where we stayed for a few days. Paul and his new friend went off to a party. In the meantime, I had met this very good-looking guy, and we were supposed to meet that evening in town. The plan was that he would take me over to the party, so I could hook up with Paul. I didn't speak Spanish, but I managed to take a bus into the city to the square where we were to meet.

Unfortunately, he never showed up. I didn't have a phone number or the address of where the party was. So, I walked through the city, trying to find a bus to take me back. It had turned dark and was getting late. Finally, a cab appeared out of nowhere! I got in and then tried to explain to the driver that I was trying to find my friends who had gone to a party. The driver spoke very little English. I was so scared that I would be lost forever. But, eventually, after we drove around for a while, I recognized the car of our friend and found them. That was a true miracle!

At the party we met some other Americans from Illinois. Their father owned a newspaper, and they were traveling around for several months, a brother, sister, and friend. They were going to head down to the coast to Puerto Escondido and said I could come along with them since they had room in their jeep. Paul decided that I would be safe with them, and that he would head back home to Baltimore. So we parted ways; he went north and I headed south to Oaxaca en route to the ocean with my new friends.

Once in Puerto Escondido I rented a house for four dollars a month. It sat on the hill above the Pacific Ocean. The house had one room with a dirt floor. The small back end of the room had three grass and mud walls and a grass-thatched roof. The front part of the room had no walls, just two poles that held up a hammock. The hammock was my bed. There was a little outhouse, also made of grass and mud. It had no door, no toilet, and just a dirt floor. Since the pigs ran wild through the community, they kept everything clean. One spigot at the top of the hill had running water for people to go and fill their buckets.

The lady next to me would make beans and tortillas for breakfast every morning, and I would pay her a few pesos. I'd walk down the hill to the beach and spend the day there. I tried to be back at my house before dark because I didn't have my glasses and feared I wouldn't be able to find my house. Sure enough, one night I didn't make it back before dark. I walked around for a very long time, trying to find my place. I was walking right by it but couldn't see it. Finally, I accidentally stumbled upon it. Divine intervention again!

One day I met a very nice Italian fisherman on the beach. Luciano was so nice and very polite. He invited me to stay and have dinner with him by the water's edge. I did, and we had a lovely time. He walked me home afterwards and asked to see me the next day. So we met each day on the beach, and Luciano took me with him out on his little boat to catch fish. We talked for hours through his broken English. He told me about Stromboli, the beautiful Italian island in the Mediterranean where he lived. I was twenty-one, and he was thirty-one.

After several weeks, it was time for him to leave and return to Italy. He'd booked passage on a freighter ship that would take him two months to arrive home. I told him I was on my way to Europe after Mexico, so I promised that I would come and visit him. He didn't believe me. Luciano called me *chamaca* (a Mexican slang word for little girl), and said I had a very idealist view of life, which is why he'd given me that nickname.

When the day came for Luciano to leave, we had a wonderful afternoon together, and then I walked with him to the bus. He gave me a beautiful letter as only an Italian could do! He wanted so much for me to come and see his beautiful island, but he claimed that life would never be that good to him, that life would happen, and I would never show up. However, just in case, he'd included

$150.00 to help with expenses, should I find my way to Italy.

Well, I was just stubborn enough that I was going to prove him wrong. I'd get there if it killed me. So, the next day I packed up, hopped on the bus, and was off to Merida (in the Yucatan), so I could fly home to Miami. Once I arrived in Merida, I went straight to the airport, not knowing the airport was closed at night. I thought airports were open 24/7. So the cab that brought me there brought me to a nearby hotel. I couldn't pay for a night's lodging and an airplane ticket, so I went into the little hotel, hoping that I'd be able to sit in the lobby until morning. The man behind the desk refused my request, but said I was welcome to sleep in his bed in the back. It was clear what he wanted, so I left and took the cab back to the airport. I hid in the bushes next to the airport door until daylight when the airport opened again.

Once I arrived in Miami, Mom asked if I would stay for a couple of weeks, so I could help her move back to Chattanooga. I agreed. I loaded the truck and drove it back to Tennessee for her. While I was there, she and my sister, Judy, who'd been living with Mom, got into a screaming argument. Judy was pregnant for the second time (with no husband in sight). She hadn't told Mom. In Miami, she'd worked night shift, and kept out of Mom's way. The rest of the time she wore long sweaters to hide her swelling belly.

As the fight escalated, Mom informed Judy that she would not support another child—that Judy would have to move out and support herself. That's when my sister screamed, "Well, you had a baby out of wedlock!" And that's when I learned about Steve Sergeant's baby and the rest of the lies.

Staying with Luciano in Stromboli

Having helped move Mom like she asked, I figured my time was running out, so a couple of weeks later, I flew off to Europe with fifty dollars and a return ticket in my pocket.

Once the plane was circling to land in Brussels, I thought, *What am I going to do now?* I had no plans and very little money, so I started talking with an American guy who was also hitchhiking. We ended up traveling together, camping out along the way. We traveled through the Black Forest and into France. It didn't take long for me to realize that my funds were going fast, so I decided I better start heading to Italy.

I called Luciano before boarding a train to Switzerland. He'd just arrived home the day before and told me to take the train to Rome. He said he'd drive there to meet me. His sister lived there and would put us up. Luciano and I had a wonderful time. He took me around, showing me sights all over Rome, as well as the Vatican. Then we drove to Naples, to his family's home. I stayed with them for a week, and then we boarded the ship for Stromboli.

Sicily is the boot of Italy, and there are seven small islands north of Sicily referred to as the Aegean Islands. Stromboli was the most northern of the chain. The ship arrived once a week at 5:00 a.m. The whole village came down to the shore to see who was arriving. It was the excitement of the week. There was no dock, so the ship anchored out from shore. The village men would climb in their little wooden fishing boats and row out to the side of the ship. We climbed down a rope ladder into a boat and they rowed us to shore. The other men and women would grab hold of the chain from the boat and pull it up on shore and then help us climb out.

Stromboli is a small island in the Mediterranean Sea. It has an active volcano and a population of about fifty people. There's no running water, no cars, no industry, and no TV. Some people had refrigerators or cook tops powered by bottle gas. A few had little make-shift carts pulled by mopeds. Except when needing to haul things in these little carts, everyone walked. The island had sandy, black beaches from the volcanic ash. About two thirds of the way up the volcano were little yellow flowers. They were everywhere. Life in Stromboli was peaceful and slow.

There was one bakery, and I'd walk there and buy bread fresh out of the stone ovens. No one grew vegetables, so anything you ate had to be brought in by boat. Another option was to take a day trip to the next island in the Aegean chain, so that you could purchase meat and vegetables. No one spoke English, and Luciano's English was very broken, so long conversations were out of the question, except when tourists visited the island. Then I would talk their heads off.

Luciano bought a villa facing the sea in hopes that I would stay with him. The second-story bedroom had huge wooden doors with smaller doors inside them that you could open. These doors opened onto a balcony that overlooked the Mediterranean Sea. The house was enclosed by a courtyard and garden trees. All the houses there were made of twelve inch thick walls and washed white. One day, sitting on the beach, I read a book on existentialism. As I turned the pages, the author was making the point that as humans, we need to have something to believe in, so we create gods to fill that need. Well, that was the first time I was presented with an idea that cast doubt on the deity of my God! I pondered the statement and thought, *What do I have to lose if this man's argument is true? I decided I had nothing to lose, but that I'd have a lot to lose if it wasn't—like my soul!* Still, in my heart of hearts, I knew God was my friend—that He was still watching over me, even as I made mistake after mistake.

As fall approached and the weather began to cool, I knew it wouldn't be fun being there in the winter with nothing to do. My entertainment was lying on the beach, sunning, scuba diving from our small boat, water skiing, and just enjoying the water. None of this would be possible when the cool weather came. I also knew something else in my heart of hearts: that I wasn't called to be a barefoot, pregnant, fisherman's wife. I knew it before I went there, and I knew it as I made plans to leave.

After returning to the States, I ended up in Chattanooga, training at Hutcheson Hospital to become a Medical Technologist. The class was very small that year, and there were only two women, me and another woman named Mary. I was twenty-one, and Mary was thirty-one. We did not look like twins. She had long, red hair and freckles, and her attire solely consisted of dresses that were almost to her ankles. She never wore makeup, and didn't believe in cutting her hair, either. She was a Bible-toting Church of God poster child. I, on the other hand, had just returned from bumming around the world—no bra, minimal clothing, and no shoes most of the time.

Now I had to spend eight hours a day in a building with no windows! I was confined to white uniforms, the old-fashioned, hard-soled nurse's shoes that had to be laced up. And I had to wear panty hose.

The class was difficult, so for survival, Mary and I bonded very quickly. She was a very nice person, married, and a mom to two teenage daughters. Early on, Mary decided I needed redemption, so I became her project. She'd never met anyone like me.

One Monday morning, she came to school with a black New Testament. She said the Lord had told her during church last night to give it to me. "If I give it to you, will you read it?" she asked. I said of course. That night as I lay in my bed, I started at the beginning, Matthew, chapter one. It was the first time I'd read the Bible as an adult. It was like reading a novel this time, except that it was the story of humanity.

Every night I would read. When I got to the story of the wheat and the tares, I had an awakening. I realized that God was trying to give me something wonderful, and I'd let all the religious hypocrites keep me from receiving all He had. I used to be very stubborn, so I decided that there was no way I was going to let that happen. I planned to go back to church one more time.

I called my sister, Judy, and asked if my two-year-old niece, Dawn, could spend Saturday night with me, and she agreed. I picked Dawn up in the afternoon, and we went shopping. I bought her a beautiful, very expensive, pink dress. The next morning I dressed her up like a doll and off we went to St. Elmo Presbyterian Church (since it was the closest church to my apartment). The most amazing thing happened. The roof did not fall in! And I've been in church ever since that day.

1974: Marriage--Loss of Dreams and Expectations

I started dating at fifteen, and several guys had bought me engagement rings in hopes that I would marry them. But something inside me knew that I wasn't supposed to do that. Soon after returning home from Europe, I became engaged to a young man named Jeff.

We went to talk with a pastor of a small satellite church of First Presbyterian. Early on in the conversation, he realized Jeff wasn't saved, so he presented the plan of salvation. Jeff nodded and said all the right things. I sat there, thinking, *Wow! This is great!*

Then we got in the car and drove off. Jeff made the statement, "What a load of ----!"

I was shocked. "If you didn't believe it, why didn't you say that all that stuff doesn't make any sense?"

"Because I knew if I did, he wouldn't marry us."

At that moment I knew I couldn't go through with this marriage. I prayed for God to help me have the courage and the words that would allow me to walk away. He did, and Jeff and I parted ways. About six months later, he committed suicide.

So when I met my first husband, I had some trepidation. He was a genius, handsome, with long eyelashes and almond-shaped eyes. He'd been in the Air Force. And he wanted to marry me after only three weeks of dating. I made it really clear to my first husband that my life was about serving the Lord and that He had called me to the mission field. If he didn't want to fill his life with God and attend my church with me, then there was no reason for us to marry. That was one of the few times I communicated my needs.

My first husband assured me, that oh yes, that was exactly what he wanted. So I believed him. He kept pushing me to marry him on his birthday, October 20th. I wasn't in any rush, since we'd only known each other for twenty-one days! But he was persistent, constantly pushing for this perfect birthday present, so I thought the key to his backing off would be my requirement for him to meet with my pastor. If Brother Ken, in all his spiritual knowledge, blessed our union, then I would marry my first husband. You see, my first husband was Catholic, and I attended an Independent Baptist Church at that time. I assumed that my pastor would have numerous reasons not to marry us. Surely, at least, he would kindly tell my first husband the sensible thing was to wait.

The church was across the street from my Cousin Ruth's house, so I stayed there while my first husband met with Brother Ken. I gave the meeting little thought because I was so certain of the outcome. Several hours later Brother Ken and my first husband arrived at the house. Cheerful words rang out from Brother Ken's mouth, "Nancy, you may look all over the world, but I don't believe that you'll find a better man! You have my blessings!"

Completely shocked, I began to cry, running into the bedroom. Everyone thought I was crying because I was happy, but I was crying because I felt trapped and didn't know how to escape. That was a Thursday night.

My next tactic was to say I wanted a church wedding, and if he could get all the paperwork done before Sunday, I'd do it. To my surprise, he did. I found myself going to look for wedding dresses after work on Friday night. I found a long, white wedding dress and veil that fit perfectly on my tiny little body. The women of the church found out that I was getting married that Sunday afternoon at 3:30, so they put together a reception for me, and my cousin bought our wedding cake. I was supposed to leave for a tour of Israel on a Monday morning, but instead I got married the day before.

I remember standing in the back of the church thinking, "What are you doing? You don't even know this guy!" I wanted to run out the back door, but I felt like I had to go through with it because of all the things the ladies in my church had done to make it happen. I knew on the honeymoon I wouldn't be riding off into the sunset.

And that was the loss of my dreams, expectations, and hopes for what marriage would be like. You see the person I dated and the person I married turned out to be different. We married October 20, 1974. Up till that point, I didn't know what it was like to stay in one place and have the same friends for more than a year. I didn't know stability, and it wasn't until I was married that I ever lived in any house more than a year.

In February, 1975, I became pregnant. I felt even more trapped because with a baby about to arrive, there was no way to extricate myself from that marriage. I was so miserable and angry at God. The cold winter night I found out I was pregnant, I walked out on the back porch and sat down in my flannel night gown, crying out to God, "How could you do this to me?"

My pastor would see me in the grocery store and just laugh, "Oh, Sister Nancy, you just don't know what a blessing this is from God!" Well, I didn't think it was a blessing. In fact, I was convinced that God had lost His mind. I felt He'd obviously ordained the pregnancy since my first husband and I were using two different methods of birth control. I also thought all the people around me were crazy. No one understood that I was truly not a happy camper. They all thought I was kidding. I wasn't! In my misery, I didn't allow myself to build a relationship with my baby before he was born.

The funny thing is once John was born and I held him in my arms, it was love at first sight, a love second only to God. Once I became a mother, I understood what God had sacrificed for me! That evening when they brought John to me, we were alone together. I held him in my arms and looked at his fingers and toes, and then I gave him back to God for full-time service. I knew one thing clearly: that God loaned him to me, and it was my responsibility to raise him to love God. I knew that if I ever lost sight of the fact that he belonged to God and thought he belonged to me that God would take him away.

My first husband went to church with me for the first year of our marriage, but after John was born, he said he felt as if he was spiritually dying, and that he wanted to go back to the Catholic Church.

What could I say? From then on, each Sunday, we attended separate churches.

1975: Mom Dies

I'd always felt like I raised my mom. She was like a child, and for that reason I always loved her in spite of the things she did. I knew she made so many poor choices because she was trying to fill up the hole in her heart. Even as a child, I understood somewhere within me that her actions were a result of her broken heart. I suppose that's one of the reasons I could never hate her. I knew deep down her heart was good. Even though I began working at fourteen to help support the family, no matter what I did, she never believed I loved her.

When I discuss my loss history graph, I usually share this story about my mom because it is a wonderful example of getting emotionally complete. (Emotional completeness falls into three categories: amends, forgiveness, and significant emotional statements.) After I moved back to Tennessee from Europe, I was twenty-one and working in the lab at Hutchinson Hospital. My mother ended up in the hospital, requiring surgery. She had to have artificial arteries put in to replace those that were so sclerotic. Doctors were not sure she would live through the surgery, so I stayed with her at the hospital for three days, never leaving her side.

Mom did recover, and about two weeks later, she sent me a card. It is the only thing I have of hers today. When I opened the card and read, I could hardly believe my eyes. It said, "Nancy, as I was about to go through those surgery doors, I looked up into your big green eyes, and I saw for the first time all the love that you have been trying to tell me about. I know that we have had our differences, and I apologize for my part in that. But I want you to know that I now know that you really do love me." That is exactly what she wrote.

Undelivered emotional communication usually falls into three categories. The first is apologies, those things that you need to apologize for. The second is the forgiveness category, those things that you need to forgive the other person for. The third is significant emotional statements, these are things you just want to say that don't fit into the other categories.

It's amazing that somehow my mom got it right! And from that point on, we had three years to try to build a relationship. Just when we were figuring things out and learning to communicate, she died. (She'd suffered a stroke at forty-two and was never well after that. At that point, she gave up her will to live and would pray to die.)

One day, a couple of years before she died, Mom came by my house to pick up something, and we were standing on the front porch, talking. Suddenly, I could see flames going up all around her face. I perceived that as if she didn't do something soon, she was going to end up in hell.

Mom hadn't talked about God much in our early life. She told me that I was christened in a Methodist church. The one time I do remember her taking my sister and me to church, she had just bought us new knit hats to wear. I was eight and my sister was six. Back then, you were expected to sit straight in the pew, not move at all, and certainly not talk. Well, we kept scratching our heads, and Mom would pinch me and tell me to stop. But we couldn't—our heads itched so much! So she jerked us up, took us outside, and began to whip us with a branch. Then she pulled our caps off and saw that we had lice. She never apologized.

Not long after the day I saw flames around her head, she did go to the altar to rededicate her life to Christ. So she was saved when she died, and that was a positive thing.

During the last six months of her life, Mom was very ill and had difficulty caring for herself. She'd considered moving into an assisted living place, but at the last minute, after the arrangements were approved, she changed her mind. She lived on the other side of town. I had a five-month-old baby, worked full-time, and had a husband who didn't want anything to do with my family, so it was difficult for me to look after her. When she told me she'd changed her mind, I drove over to the house with John to try to convince her to reconsider. I said everything I could think of, but she was adamant. In desperation, I cried out, "If you don't, you won't see your grandson again!" Of course, I didn't mean it; it was just a stupid statement I hoped would grab her attention. It didn't, and I left. Sadly, that was the last time she saw John because soon after that she died.

We didn't understand about Mom's angina back then, and sometimes we felt like she was playing wolf to gain attention. I often said, "One of these days it's going to be the real thing, and no one will believe you." Sure enough, that's exactly what happened.

I received a phone call one afternoon that Mom had been admitted to the hospital. I thought it was the same old thing again, so I waited till evening to visit her. After all these years of being understanding and kind, my patience had run out. I was very cool toward her, and when I left, I didn't say, "I love you."

I was leaving the next morning with my cousins to go to Florida for the weekend. The trip had been planned for months, my reward for having a baby. Before leaving that morning, I called to check on her condition, and they said she made it fine through surgery, so we left. Once we arrived, we decided to go to the beach before we checked into the hotel, so we didn't check in until about 6 p.m. There was a message for me to call home. I did, and my first husband told me to come right home because my mom was in very bad shape. I asked if she had died, and he said, "No, just come home."

I called the hospital and used my medical savvy to get someone to let me know whether I needed to hurry or not. I was told I could take my time. At that moment, I knew Mom was dead. My friends and I went to dinner, and then my cousin drove me to the airport. As you can imagine, I was left very incomplete with my mom! That was some heavy stuff to carry around, so I did my routine: I buried it! I learned a concept from Scarlett O'Hara in *Gone With the Wind.* Remember when she'd sigh and look off and say, "I'll worry about that tomorrow"? Well, that was my mantra, what I did after all painful situations. Tomorrow would come, and another tomorrow, and another, and another. I believed that if I thought about my pain that it would consume me and I wasn't sure I'd survive. I was twenty-five when my mom died.

1984: Divorce, Loss of
Dreams, Hopes, and Expectations

In 1984 my first husband and I divorced. It was a loss of my dreams, expectations, and hopes that I could make my marriage work. I was determined that my child would not have to experience a broken home. I gave that marriage every ounce of effort I could, but it takes two people to make a marriage work, and after ten years, I finally gave up.

When we have a broken heart, we run around trying to fix it, but what ends up happening is that we gravitate toward people who are also broken. Sadly, we try to have our needs met through the kind of people who couldn't possibly meet them. That's what happened with my first husband, only I didn't understand this concept back then.

Someone once told me about a study done with widowers who'd remarried. Within a year, a high number, something like 82%, were divorced. Why? They were trying to replace their loss. You can't *replace* a loss. You need to *emotionally complete* that loss, so that when you enter into a new relationship, you're not carrying around a fifty-pound weight around your leg (or heart), so to speak. When we're emotionally incomplete, we carry that baggage into new relationships, romantic or otherwise. We've all had experiences where we responded in a way that was less about the other person and clearly more about our own history. That person simply triggered something in us.

1987: I Failed My Best Friend: God

When I was a child, I'd always felt like there was a glass wall: I was on one side and my family was on the other. I felt like a non- entity. I didn't get in trouble. I loved going to school. I loved doing my homework. I never talked back to my parents in my entire life. I wasn't a problem. I felt like I simply didn't exist as far as my family was concerned.

But at ten years old, I found my best friend. And that best friend was God. The things that I've shared on this Loss History Graph are just a few of the many bad things that have happened to me. But no matter how bad the situation was, God always gave me the wisdom to survive and escape.

If it hadn't been for God, I know the situation in Hawaii (the rape and kidnapping) would've ended differently. I would've been murdered or fit for a mental institution. But I know God heard my cries, and He delivered me. I knew in my heart that it was He who'd given me the wisdom and timing of how to outsmart my kidnapper. He was my best friend; He'd never deserted me.

I was never a particularly self-righteous person, but I was convinced that there was one sin that I'd never commit because I loved the Lord too much. Well, a stance of pride leads to a fall, and several months after telling a friend that I'd never commit that sin, that's exactly what happened. And a couple of years later, in 1987, I experienced the *most painful* loss in my life.

If I could draw the line of this graph down to the center of the earth I would. I'm going to be transparent here, but I tell my clients that if they have things they're uncomfortable sharing it's all right because it's not the event that's important but the emotions attached to the event.

Up until that point, I had always been the type of person who never looked back. I didn't take the time to examine things of the past. Instead, if someone gave me a new piece of information, and it was of value to me, I grabbed on to it. I was like a sponge. I had absolutely no sympathy for people who struggled to let go of people or things, and worse, I had no compassion for those who didn't simply stop certain behaviors that weren't beneficial to them.

And then I met Mike. A friend had convinced me to go out with her to a local restaurant (that also had a dance floor). She kept daring me to ask the man on my right to dance. To get her off my back, I did. Mike was not only a great dancer, he was a great conversationalist. Also, he looked too good to be true: tall, well-built, blue eyes.

"You're married, aren't you?" I asked. And without waiting for a reply, I added, "Do you have any pictures of your kids with you?" Mike pulled out his wallet-sized pictures of his kids. His eyes were filled with love for them. So Mike (sometimes known as "Python Arms" to his buddies) and I became friends, and when he came to town, we'd go jogging. I'd tell friends, "We're *only* running partners!"

But Mike was unhappily married; he and his wife both wanted a divorce, but they were at a stalemate. She wanted $2,000 a month for child support. Even though Mike was an engineer on the railroad (between Chattanooga and Nashville), that amount wouldn't leave him enough money for his own expenses.

After several visits, it became clear that our

wonderful rapport seemed to be leading us down the dark alley of adultery. I knew it was wrong, but Mike was truly the only man I'd ever been in love with. He understood me and loved me in a way no one (but God) ever had. I think he understood me better than I understood myself.

Never before had I let any man into my heart. Only children had been allowed into my heart, because I figured they were safe, and men were not, because of what I saw growing up. It was so cool to have a friend who understood and adored me and gave eleven-year-old John all the attention he'd never been given by his own dad.

It's not that my first husband didn't love John; he did. It's just that he really didn't know how to relate to people, especially children. Ironically, Mike's children wouldn't give him the time of day. So when Mike came to town each week, John and he had a blast together. Sometimes he would stay with John when I had to work Saturdays at the hospital. I'd walk into the house, and there they'd be, nestled on the couch. Mike would have his arm propped up on the back of the sofa, and John would be right next to him. They'd be watching TV, content as could be. As a mom that loving bond was wonderful to see, but then I'd think about Mike's own children. The youngest was seven; his two others were teens: thirteen and fifteen.

Time and time again during that two-year period, I'd tell Mike that he really needed to go back to his wife and work it out. Inevitably, he'd knock on my door, crying, and I'd let him back in. All the while I knew I was failing God and bringing sorrow to my best friend. My fairy-tale relationship had a big, black cloud over it, never allowing me any real peace.

After several times of my sending Mike off to make amends with his wife, he finally agreed. He told me he'd give it his best try. I told him I was happy for him. But truthfully, I was really mad at God.

"How could You do this to me?" I cried. "You let me find out what real love is, knowing that I couldn't have it? You jerked away this kind of love!"

I wasn't mad at Mike. I was mad at God. You see, when my divorce was finalized, I'd taken off my wedding band and gone to the jewelry store and bought the most expensive diamond cross they had. I put it on my neck and never took it off. It was a reminder that I'd made a decision to never again choose a man over what God had called me to do.

The night Mike said his final good-bye, I ripped that cross off my neck and lay flat on the floor, beating my fists on the linoleum, saying, "I hate you, God! I hate you!" When I finally paused, I heard Him speak.

"When you signed on with Me, it was a one-way ticket, so get over it," God replied.

Stunned by His simple answer, I stood up, went to bed, and the next morning was up and off to work. God knew that I didn't hate Him, but in that moment, I was just angry because I didn't get my way. Letting those feelings leap up and out was my honest expression. He didn't strike me dead when I yelled at Him. I guess that's why I don't have a problem with other people getting angry with God.

Look at David. He tells God off, and then, in the telling, he comes around full circle. And that's how you come around full circle with God, by getting it up and out. That's part of the healing process.

I knew I could've had Mike if I'd wanted him; that wasn't the issue. The issue was that I had a calling on my life, and I belonged to God, and I knew in my heart of hearts that I couldn't have both, and that fact would ultimately prevent me from finding lasting happiness with Mike.

One night a few months after Mike left, I was in my apartment crying out to God, "Where are You?! Where are You?! You told me You wouldn't put more on me than I can bear and that You'd be here to help me. So I keep asking You to help remove this burden from me, but it seems You've gone off on a fishing trip or something!"

Then I heard this still, small voice say, "I will be glad to take care of it when you let me." It was then that I understood that I'd been trying to fix my hurt myself.

So I answered, "Fine! Your shoulders are bigger than mine. Let's see what You can do." This wasn't a reverential spiritual dialogue. It was more of a "Have at it, buddy!" But within six weeks, my burden was gone forever.

Still, the bottom line was that I ached because I'd spent two years failing my best friend. After He healed my emotional "open wound," I spiraled into a depression, and since my drug of choice had always been food, I began to eat myself into oblivion. I gained forty pounds in two months.

One day I was in the kitchen, and while

reaching for a glass, my hand grazed the counter, and a dirty glass broke on the floor. The next day I was in the kitchen again, reaching for a glass, and as my arm moved, another dirty glass on the counter smashed on the floor. As I observed this in slow motion, I realized I'd never cleaned up the glass from the day before. At that moment, I knew I was in trouble and had better seek some help fast.

I kept longing to go back to where I was spiritually before the whole affair happened. I now understand that experience was a huge blessing in my life. Previously, I'd lacked compassion for people who couldn't let go of things that weren't good for them. I'd been humbled, realizing all of us, no matter how much we love God, are capable of anything (even murder), given certain circumstances. Being weak is part of being human and living in this sinful world. When you're real clear on that, it's hard to judge other people. Even Simon Peter bailed out on Jesus, and he spent three years with him.

I know that God used my experience with Mike as part of the preparation I needed in my ministry. I work with so many people who have a different set of moral values than I do, but I don't judge them. I see people's broken hearts. So often when your heart is broken, you can't get to God until you've received some healing. Compassion was one of the treasures I needed to walk out my destiny. Of course, I didn't know that back then, and so I wasn't really that pleased with God.

The night following the Lord's telling me to give Him my burdens, I went to Red Bank Baptist Church for their evening service. It was January 1, the beginning of a new year. I'd never been to that church before, and I've never been there since. God prompted me to read Psalm 37:4: "Delight yourself in the things of the Lord and I will give you the desires of your heart." OK, I thought, *If that's what I'm supposed to do, God, I give you permission to fill my days and nights. I'm going to ask You to guide the rest of the journey of my life.* And slowly, I began to come out of the depression.

In the meantime, a friend from Overeaters Anonymous gave me a number to call. I called and asked if there was a program for eating disorders, and the woman on the phone began asking me questions. She said they didn't have a program for that, but there was one that started in a week that she thought would be very helpful for me. It was a seven-day, in-treatment program for co-dependency. At that time, I had no idea what co-dependency was, but I knew this program was a life-line, and I had to get there.

I drove ten hours to St. Simon Island with no idea what I was driving into. There was a group of nine women, and one day we were doing what is called "Mirror Work." The therapist had you sit in a chair in front of this full-length mirror as she dialogued with you. When my turn came, I stood in the middle of the floor, frozen solid. No matter what she said, I couldn't move—I was petrified. Thank goodness that therapist was patient, because it took quite a few minutes before she could coax me into that chair.

Once I was seated, I was told to look at myself in the mirror. I found I couldn't look directly into my eyes. I just couldn't do it. Finally, the therapist managed to get me to hold my head up and look.

Oh my! I realized that I'd never done that before. Here I'd spent a lifetime of doing my hair and make-up, but I'd avoided my eyes because I was afraid of what I would see, which probably related to my feelings of being defective.

What I saw when I looked into the mirror was astounding! My whole life I'd been the friend that you would've wanted to have. I gave 110%. I stood by all my friends, in spite of their choices. What I saw was the friend I'd been searching for, the true friend, and I'd treated the little girl in me ten times worse than anyone ever had. I made a commitment that day to start taking care of myself.

Several other interesting things happened during that week, but one seemed especially significant. One lady was doing her anger work on her abusive ex-husband. She had terrible back problems, so when it came time for her to take the bat and beat the pillows to free up everything she was feeling, she said she couldn't do it because it would worsen her back. The therapist looked at me and asked if I would stand in for her. I didn't have a clue what was going on, but I agreed. (That was usual for me back then, not to have a clue, but to jump in anyway.) So I stood up and started pounding that pillow with the bat. And everything that lady felt came pouring out of my mouth. Afterwards, she told me I'd said absolutely everything that was in her heart! She said there was no way she could've done a better job. The group was flabbergasted and so was I. The whole thing seemed surreal. The lady and I ended up friends, and I would visit her for years until she died.

On the last day we had a little graduation party. We sat on the floor and the therapist said something about each of us and gave us a pair of "angel wings." When she got to me, she said, "Nancy, there are few people who have natural counseling gifts, but you are one. You'd make a wonderful therapist!"

Well, you could've knocked me over with a feather. I was more than stunned. Surgeon, yes; therapist, no way! I was a Medical Technologist, and for over twenty years I'd worked in a laboratory. The way I saw it: things were black and white. The one doll I had as a child had a figure like a Barbie. I used to pretend she was a brain surgeon named Dr. Diamond. I was thirty-eight, and being a therapist had never entered my mind.

One of the things I learned from that program was what "boundaries" meant. During the first few days, the therapist kept throwing that word around, but I wasn't sure what she meant, and since the word wasn't twenty-six letters long, I was too embarrassed to ask. She mentioned it enough that I realized I needed to understand the concept. So that night, I asked my roommate what "boundaries" meant. I guess that tells you we didn't have any in my childhood home.

John was an only child, and I loved doing things for him. It brought me great pleasure. So back at home, I decided to put my new skills to use. I made a sign and hung it above the kitchen door. It read, "Self-service Kitchen."

When John came home from school that day, he saw the sign and just shook his head. That evening, we were watching TV, and John said,

"Mom, I sure would like to have a Coke." I realized this was my chance to practice my new skills. I paused, groping for words in my mind as to what I would say. "You know," I replied. "I would, too. Would you mind getting me one while you're up?"

I'll never forget the look on his face as long as I live. He turned his head slightly as his mouth fell open in shock. I repeated my statement. He shook his head and walked to the kitchen and brought me a Coke. Later that night, I said, "I'm going to the kitchen, do you want anything?" You see, we teach people how to treat us; that's the point of boundaries. And indeed, if we teach then, we can re-teach them, and that is what I did.

I grew so much during that time of grappling with the pain of losing Mike and knowing I'd failed God, but here are a few other things I learned:

1. That God is *always* with me, no matter what I'm doing.

2. That the Holy Spirit continues to try to draw a person back from sin, even when that person's trying to plug up her ears.

3. Our Heavenly Bridegroom provides the ultimate love story, the perfect love story. In the midst of my loss, I'd discovered the heart of God and my Heavenly Bridegroom, and when I allowed God's presence to fill up all the spaces in *my heart*, I learned that earthly attachments wouldn't fill that longing, only God could.

Early into my marriage with my first husband, I'd told him, "If I ever get rid of you, I'm not going to get another one." What I meant was I didn't need another child to look after. I've always been independent. I had God, my son, and my career. *Wasn't that enough?* I wondered. About six years after Mike left, I was driving and listening to a Christian radio station. A man was saying we had to trust God with *everything*. And at that moment I was convicted of not trusting God with my marital status. So I made a pact with God. I told Him that I would be open, but I wasn't going out, looking for a husband. If He wanted me to have someone, then He would have to put that man in my face. I thought I was so smart! But, as usual, God one-upped me. Through a series of events, I met Tony, a man eleven years my senior and, in some ways, my exact opposite. I like to do things on the spur of the moment, and Tony likes to plan. When I met Tony, I watched everything he did, waiting for the skeletons to come tumbling out of his closet. But they never did. He is the most consistent person I've ever met. He treats everyone with respect. His parents were married sixty-five years until they died, and made goo-goo eyes at each other up until the end.

After a few times of being in Tony's company, the Lord told me plainly that I was to marry him. "This is My will for your life, Nancy." And that's what I did. I just trusted God that He knew best, and, of course, he did. Tony brought me stability and a faithful, deep love beyond anything I could have imagined. Even though he was baptized at nine, I brought him a new way to think about and experience God. Together, we have grown a lot.

Once I made a list of all the men I'd ever dated in my life to ascertain the common denominator. At first, it was hard to find a connection. There were all kinds of men, from hippies to bank executives, from poor guys to millionaires. The first thing I saw was that my first boyfriend and Tony both loved me very much, and we had great friendships. The rest, I realized, were all "emotionally out to lunch" like my daddy. Of course, all those years, what I wanted more than anything else was to feel emotionally connected. But, unconsciously, I kept creating what was familiar until I did the work of Grief Recovery® and became emotionally complete with my dad.

1990: Diagnosed with a Terminal Illness

In 1990, I was diagnosed with a terminal illness and was told that I had about two years to live. The stresses in my life had accumulated, and because I had just "stuffed down" my pain, my immune system became impaired. The extreme stress had brought forth my genetic predisposition for systemic sclerosis. My diagnosis was a loss of my dreams, expectations, and hopes for the goals I had for my future. At first, I wasn't sure I wanted to put my diagnosis on my Loss History Graph, because as it turned out, my sickness has been one of the greatest things to ever happen to me. I know such a statement needs an explanation.

My sickness was a crucial stage that led me to my current calling. It helped me to let go of all things in my life that weren't so important. I changed my priorities and became a "big picture" thinker.

Since God had delivered me from all my other "bad" situations, I never questioned him about the grim end my doctors were predicting. I never said, "Why me, God?" During the first month of my diagnosis, I felt deeply sad for one reason: I so enjoyed spending time with my son, John, and the idea that we wouldn't have years and years ahead brought an ache to my heart. But after that month, peace just settled over me. I figured that whatever lay in the future must be something worse than my sickness, and God, in His omniscient kindness, was trying to spare me from it.

I trusted God with my life and never prayed for healing. He'd already proven to me, time and time again, that He had my best interests in mind. It's not that I didn't have brief prayer times, it's just that I'm not geared for these long, drawn out prayer sessions. I figured if I told God something once that ought to be enough. I mean He's obviously intelligent; He knows what I need. So my prayer life was more of an ongoing dialogue with a best friend. Driving proved a fruitful time to talk with God. The older I've become, the easier it's been to hear His voice. When I was younger, I just felt His presence, and somehow knew when He was trying to communicate with me. I felt inclinations to do this or that; I wasn't aware of His actual words.

I've never put God in a box, but there are plenty of Christians who want to put Him in a box that they've designed based on their earthly concept of what spirituality is. So they keep looking for Him in that box. True joy comes from serving Him in His Kingdom. That's the place where we fall madly in love with Him and can see beyond earthly dimensions. It's that other world that's reserved for those who diligently seek Him. Psalm 42:8 says He sings over us during the night. I wish I'd known that earlier in my life!

So my simple prayer to God during this time was my heart attitude: whatever You want is best.

I figured this illness was just something I was supposed to walk out. I was in pain ninety-five percent of the time. I couldn't walk ten feet without gasping for air because the pain was so intense. When it was excruciating beyond words, I'd just close my eyes and pray, "Jesus, Jesus, Jesus," over and over until I fell asleep. Often, I'd lie in a hammock I'd brought back from Mexico, visualizing God's arms around me.

When I started graduate school at Vanderbilt, I was still in pain and on a very high dose of Procardia (90 mg.), a vasodilator drug used to keep my arteries open. The average dose is 15-30 mg. When I finished school, I moved back, married Tony, and experienced a time of improvement. I used to take Prednisone tapers every two months, but then there started to be longer periods between the doses. And then suddenly, I would begin to go downhill again. Certain things would begin to happen. I was a Hospice nurse and did home health visits. I'd start out at 9:00 a.m., and then it'd be 11:00 a.m., and I hadn't yet arrived at my first appointment. I would just keep driving as my energy evaporated and my brain slowed down. Often, I couldn't even think, "Just go home!" I would wander around in a daze. That's how I knew the systemic sclerosis was coming on, and soon afterwards, when the deteriorating arteries would go into spasm, scar tissue would then form on the outside of the arterial walls, causing pain, and preventing oxygen from reaching my tissues.

At one point I was sent to Vanderbilt to be evaluated for a research study. It took several months before it was time for my appointment. I had copies of all my medical records and took those with me. I met with the Head of the

Department of Rheumatology. He examined me, looked at my records, and walked out of the room to consult with his associate. Then he returned to the room, shaking his head, saying, "I can't explain this. When I look at your records and your body, they don't match. You shouldn't be alive, and since you are, your body doesn't appear to have the severe organ damage that goes with this disease. I just can't explain this!"

I looked at Tony, and he looked at me. We both knew that God had taken His hand and put a hold on my condition. He didn't completely take away my pain, but I knew He was preserving my life because He had something for me to do.

After that, my pain began to decrease, and the time between steroids increased. Now, I'm in pain only about five percent of the time. I take 30 mg. of Procardia and haven't needed steroids in fifteen months. Why I tell all this is because I saw a direct correlation between doing my emotional healing and enjoying physical improvement. The more I "cleaned out the pot," the fewer symptoms I had. I was four years into my illness when I learned about Grief Recovery®, but as soon as I did that work, my symptoms improved dramatically. Today you see so many women with Fibromyalgia and chronic fatigue syndrome; those are autoimmune diseases. I've seen women who were immobilized watch their symptoms decrease significantly or disappear completely just by doing Grief Recovery® work. They are able to go back to work and start living again.

1993: Empty Nest

When it was time for John to go off to college, I

knew I was going to be in trouble. I always used to say he was my rose in the middle of the desert. We've been best friends since he was three. We'd pile up in bed and play role reversal. He'd act like the parent, and I'd act like the kid. We just had a blast.

When my first husband and I divorced, we lived on Signal Mountain, amidst doctors and lawyers, in a large, beautiful house. John was ten, and I thought to myself, *Do I want my son to remember that we had a nice house in a nice neighborhood, or do I want to make memories with my child?* I knew in order to keep that house and lifestyle, I was going to have to work more hours, so I opted for the memories, and we walked away from everything. We moved to the bottom of the mountain into a two-bedroom apartment.

After about a month, John said, "Mom, have you noticed what's different about being here?"

"Yes," I said. "It's quiet! Pretty neat, isn't it?" He agreed, smiling. You see, as soon as we walked into the apartment, we took off our shoes. My first husband had never allowed us to go without our shoes in the house. He said we'd catch a cold. My first husband was the Head of Radiology at a children's hospital, so he knew that colds come from viruses, not from going barefoot. Another freedom John and I enjoyed was putting on our pajamas, piling up on the couch, and eating cereal for supper. We thought we were at camp. It was so much fun.

I can't remember us ever arguing. I can't stand whining kids, so I started him out right. I told him that I would tell him one time to do something. If I had to repeat myself, he knew he was going to be in severe trouble. And when I said a subject was closed, it was closed. He knew I meant business, and that's the way it was, and he respected me. Sometimes my first husband would ask me, "Why doesn't John mind me as well as he does you?!"

When John was a teenager, his friends would come over all the time, and I was John's mom to all the guys. It was nothing to pile them up in the car and head to Florida for the weekend. We always had fun! I loved being John's mom. It filled up my life.

Since he was born, however, we knew he was going to college; that was the plan. One day, maybe a month before he was to leave, I was taking a nap and woke with a start. My heart was about to beat out of my chest, and I couldn't get my breath. The relationship between a parent and a child seems to have an invisible umbilical cord. And when I woke up from that nap, I felt like someone had taken a knife and cut that cord in two, and for the first time since he'd come into my life, I felt like we were separated. I was here, and he was over there. I thought I was dying from the pain. Then I realized I was having a panic attack. We'd never had that separation before. When Tony and I began dating, he said, "I can't believe you two are mother and son; you seem like brother and sister!" We've just always enjoyed each other.

At the end of the summer of 1993, I helped John move into his dorm room at Tennessee Tech. We finished about 11:30 p.m. I then drove over to Nashville and started my graduate program at Vanderbilt the next day. We laugh and say we went off to college together.

Our relationship changed, and it needed to. It was time for John to spread his wings. Grappling with my illness and going to school didn't relieve the loss of an "empty nest." All those daily moments with John had made life such a joy, and separating was a punch to my heart.

2007: Discover My Father Died

The last and most recent loss came through a phone conversation with my father's wife in March during which I learned that he'd died back in September. I was shocked, saddened, and disappointed. The next chapter about the Relationship Graph examines our history in greater detail.

CHAPTER 11
GRIEF RECOVERY ACTION 2
THE RELATIONSHIP GRAPH

Once you've completed your Loss History Graph, the next major step is to identify a relationship that you want to emotionally complete. Because losses and pain occur in the context of relationships, it's vital to complete the pain and losses in an important relationship, and to do that we need to create an accurate picture of the relationship. Then, and only then, can we deal with the pain and issues that need to be completed.

The directors of The Grief Recovery® Institute teach that in order to recreate an accurate memory-picture of a relationship, it's helpful to use a clear-cut format. Those of us who lead Grief Recovery® training seminars have developed an extremely simple process that has had amazing results in helping individuals discover what is unfinished for them in significant relationships.

In the Loss History Graph, we focus on loss. We

write about sad, painful, or negative life events that we remember. That graph includes many different people. The point of the Relationship Graph is to take a comprehensive and very detailed look at one relationship.[59] The Relationship Graph is designed to aid a very natural process. The authors of *The Grief Recovery Handbook* point out that:

> At some point after a loss occurs, our brains begin a review, searching for what we never communicated or completed. You may or may not be aware that this review began very soon after the loss. In fact, the review continues intermittently until the loss is completed. The purpose of the Relationship Graph is to help you tap into that review and use it to discover what is unfinished for you so that you can then complete it."[60]

When we do The Relationship Graph, positive events are marked above the center line, and negative events below the line.[61] We ask participants to make sure there are at least two events above the centerline and two events below the center line, or it'll be difficult to complete the pain in the relationship. Why? Because we must be able to tell the emotional truth about the relationship, and we can't tell the emotional truth about anyone that we've enshrined or bedeviled.

To enshrine someone is to put a person on a pedestal and believe that he or she never did or does anything wrong. To bedevil someone is to believe that person never did or does anything right. We can't have a real relationship with anyone that we've enshrined or bedeviled. The scriptural concept of honoring your father and mother may be misapplied to encourage enshrining. Self-pity, anger, and hate can lead us to bedeviling. Don't worry if, at first, you feel a "mental block," delaying you from remembering any negative experiences with a much-loved spouse or relative. Be patient.

The Relationship Graph is a tool for doing what David talked about in Psalm 51:6: "Behold, You desire truth in the innermost being, and in the hidden part You will make me know wisdom."[62] God can make us know wisdom through the revelatory power of the Holy Spirit and the through the direct application of the Word of God. The Relationship Graph is a tool that the Holy Spirit can use to help us in the process of discovery!

I share my relationship graph with my father as an example to help clients construct theirs.

My Relationship Graph: Dad

When it was time for me to do my relationship graph in the Grief Recovery® certification class, Russell sent us back to the hotel to do it as our homework assignment. We were to find at least two things above the line and two below the line. I sat on the bed for over an hour, and I couldn't find anything above the line. I became upset because I'm an over-achiever, and I was determined to complete this stupid graph! I don't have access to a lot of my memories. The ones I've found, I worked very hard for. Finally, I discovered one positive memory which then helped me discover some more, four to be exact. I was excited.

Usually you start the relationship graph at the moment you knew the other person existed on this planet. I start mine in 1950, the year I was born.

1950: I Was Born

There was a story repeatedly told in my family. Since I never knew life without the story, all of my conscious memory was filtered through its painful, underlying message.

My father was stationed in Okinawa when I was born. He arrived home a week later, walked into the house and asked, "What do you have over there in that basinet?"

"A little girl!" Mom answered.

"Well, I'll be damned!" Dad exclaimed. And he and my grandfather, so it was told, went out on a drinking binge and didn't come home until the next morning.

It's not the idea that they may have gotten drunk that was wounding, because frankly, I doubt that happened. My grandmother was a teetotaler, and she would've killed my grandfather. It's the next part of the story that stuck with me, the part which has been confirmed by other family members. It was a week before my dad even gazed into the basinet to see what I looked like because I was a girl!

So I grew up believing that I was defective. It affected my entire life until I did Grief Recovery® work and became emotionally complete with my dad. Growing up I became an overachiever in an effort to earn my dad's approval. I also had to prove that there wasn't anything on this planet a man could do that I couldn't do better. Do you think that might have affected my adult relationships? You bet! I was pretty intimidating to guys. I'd spent years earning higher degrees (collecting pieces of paper, I called it), so that I would feel better about myself. Thank goodness I don't have to chase that rat anymore, thanks to the Grief Recovery® process.

1956: Positive Event—My First Birthday Party

My mom decided to give me my first birthday party when I turned six. My birthday is on Christmas day, and my mom knew that most of the children wouldn't be able to come because they wouldn't have money for a present at Christmas time. Besides, military families didn't have much money in the first place. So when Mom sent out invitations, at the bottom she wrote, "Come for cake and ice cream, but do not bring presents." She thought that would work, but she was wrong.

The party was to be several days before Christmas, but that morning one by one the kids knocked on the door and said, "My mom said I couldn't come to the party." By eleven there was no one. So my mom called my dad and told him what happened. He instructed her to cook extra food.

That evening my dad brought home six other hulking Marines to make up for the children who couldn't attend. Do you know how big a Marine is to a six year old? We lived in basic housing on the base, and the rooms were like cracker boxes. So those men filled our entire living room! When I discovered that memory, I thought perhaps I couldn't have been that bad, since my dad did something so nice for me. My dad was 6'2" and very handsome. I had a picture of him in his uniform on the dresser in my room. I built this imaginary image of my dad that did not look anything like him.

1962: Dad Refused to Take Us

In 1962, my father was going to take me and my middle sister, Judy, to visit him for two weeks in the summer. We'd never done that before, and I was so excited about the opportunity to be with him. At the same time, my mom was taking my dad back to court to have child support increased. (Dad gave her eighty dollars per month for three children, and that was only because the government took it out of his check.) My mom worked on the curb at Krystal and made twenty dollars a week. Even back then, it wasn't enough to feed three children, my mom, and my grandmother. My dad wasn't really concerned because he figured that the judge would side with him since they were both men. The plan was for him to pick us up when he came down for the court hearing.

This is one of the most vivid memories I have of my childhood. I was sitting on the sofa with my bag packed beside me, waiting for him to come. I can't tell you how excited I was. It was one of those times when it seemed like an eternity before he showed up. When he came walking through the door, I almost jumped off the couch. I was ready. He looked at me and said, "Well, your damn mother won, so you can unpack your bag! I'm not taking you anywhere. As far as I'm concerned, you all can go to hell!" And he walked out. Can you imagine how crushed I was?

After that we didn't have a lot of contact with him, and on the rare occasions that we did, it was usually a bad experience. There are lots and lots of negative things I could recall, but what I needed to find while doing this graph were some positive events. So I will not belabor the negative. I know them in living color. However, I will share one with you, so that you can see how my memories "went to hell in a hand basket"—meaning I'd lost the positive ones and only had access to the negative ones.

At one point we were living in Miami in a one-bedroom apartment. My mom and youngest sister slept on twin beds in the bedroom. My middle sister slept on the sofa, and I slept on a twin bed in the corner of the dining room. At the same time my father had remarried. His new wife had a child from a previous marriage. They lived in Northern Virginia, and her daughter attended an affluent school for the officer's children. She was voted the best dressed child in the school, and for her sixteenth birthday, not her mother, but my father, bought her a brand new Firebird! This act of incredible generosity in light of how little he gave to me emotionally and financially inspired great resentment.

1970: Airport

In 1970, as I was heading to Europe, I decided that I'd stop and see my father on the way. I arrived in Quantico and called my dad. He came to pick me up at the bus station. He was nice to me, and for the only time in my life, he acted genuinely concerned. He didn't want me to go off to Europe by myself. He offered to help me find a job or help me go back to school. But when you are nineteen and have a ticket to Europe, you just have to go. I stayed a couple of days with him, but didn't take him up on his offer.

When it was time for me to catch my flight, he took me to the airport. This was a significant memory for me. As we got out of the car and I stepped up on the sidewalk, I reached out and took my father's hand. We walked into the airport holding hands and stayed that way until it was time for me to board the plane. That detail is important because it's the only time I could remember my father ever touching me.

1972: Dad Didn't Want Me In His House

In 1972, as I was leaving Europe, I began thinking about the offer my dad made. I decided that if I went back to Virginia, we could have a chance to build a relationship. So that became my destination. When I arrived, I called my dad and asked him to come pick me up at the bus station. He did, and all the way to his house, he never said a word. (This in itself was not unusual because my family didn't communicate.)

When he pulled up in front of the house he said, "How long are you going to be here because I really don't want you in my house." Normally, I would've said fine and walked off, but I was in a strange town and had no money, so I had to go in. At least I thought I did. Back then I didn't know that people actually sleep on the streets. His wife heard me talking to some friends on the phone. These friends lived in California and wanted me to help out with a project they were doing for disabled children. She went to my dad and said, "I bet if you buy her a ticket to San Francisco, she'll leave." So my dad offered to buy me a plane ticket. I asked if he would arrange the ticket so that I could stop in Chattanooga to visit my mom, and he agreed.

After arriving in Chattanooga, I applied for medical technology school and was accepted, so I never made it to California. One night after I graduated and was working third shift in the lab, I had a strange feeling that I needed to call my father. It was around 8:00 p.m. when I picked up the phone and called. His wife answered the phone and said that he wasn't in. I asked where he was, and she told me he was in the hospital. I asked why she hadn't called me, and she replied, "It is none of your business," and hung up. Well, I decided it was some of my business. I called the lab and told them I had to go to Virginia to check on my dad. I drove all night and arrived the next morning.

At the hospital, I discovered that he'd had open heart surgery twice in one week. When I walked into his room, he seemed very happy to see me. We actually had a conversation. (Three or four sentences! That was big for us.) I had on an engagement ring, and he asked who I was going to marry and where I worked. He said, "I want you to go over to the shop (his wife owned a hair salon in town), and get the key to the house. I want you to stay there. "Well, when I heard that, my relationship antenna went up! I thought, *His near-death experience has finally changed him!*

I drove over to the salon. When I walked in and his wife saw me she said, "What the hell are you doing in this town? You're not welcome here!" Since I'm not the type to argue with people when they've made up their minds and are quite angry, I turned around and walked out. What was I to do now? I couldn't go back and tell my dad, who was in intensive care, and get him upset. So I drove around until I came up with a solution.

I headed back to the hospital and told my dad that I'd called work and that they'd told me that if I was not at work that night, I wouldn't have a job. So I left, and he never knew the truth.

1975: John Was Born

In 1975, my son was born. I thought, "Finally, my dad will have the son he always wanted!" Wrong! I sent him a telegram and told him all about his new grandson. And except for the one event I will include here, he never acknowledged the child existed. No card, call, or anything.

When John was ten, it dawned on me one day that if the two of them passed on the street, they wouldn't even know they were related. How sad is that? I decided that it was about time for some communication, so I called my dad and explained that I wanted the two of them to meet, that we would be coming to visit.

When we arrived, Dad was nice to both of us. He took us fishing. In the only picture I have of my son and father together, John is holding the first fish he ever caught. Before we left my dad said, "When you come back, I'm going to take you and show you where I work." And, of course, my relationship antenna sprang up again!

In the meantime, I experienced the worst loss in my life, and as you might recall, my drug of choice was food. I gained about forty pounds in two months. We were scheduled to visit my dad the second week in August, as soon as John's swim meets were over.

Part of me knew I shouldn't go. But you know how, when you haven't wised up, you keep repeating the same behaviors over and over, hoping they'll have a different outcome? Well, I held tight to the side of hope. I knew my dad judged people by how much money they earned, what their social status was, and how they looked. I knew that, but I went anyway.

When we arrived at his house, he didn't want to have anything to do with me. He gave his wife a fifty-dollar bill and said, "Take them to the beach and feed them, so that I won't have to be seen in public with her." I didn't want to go to the beach; I wanted to build a relationship with my dad. But it seemed, once again, that it wasn't an option.

After we returned from the beach, I went upstairs to wash and change. When I came walking down the stairs, I could see my dad sitting in the recliner, flicking through the TV channels. My son was just sitting on the sofa.

This picture of non-communication and non-love burned in front of my eyes. The whole time we'd been there, my father had never acknowledged that my son existed. As I looked at them I was suddenly right back in the 1950s. I was in our old house, and I could feel the icicles in the room! I realized he was doing the same thing to my son that he'd done to me.

My son had never been exposed to this kind of dysfunction, and I could tell he didn't particularly relish it, so I went back upstairs and packed our bags. I came down and said, "John, we have to go now." John got up off the couch, and we walked out of the door and drove off. My dad never looked away from the TV. That was the last time I ever saw or spoke to him.

I knew my dad's post office box number, so when my son graduated from high school, I sent him an invitation. Because John was an excellent swimmer, he went to McCallie in Chattanooga. As it was a very prestigious private school that my dad knew about, I thought maybe he would be impressed enough to acknowledge John, and his accomplishment. Wrong! No response came. When I graduated from college and graduate school, he was notified, but again, he never responded.

So that is my relationship graph with my dad. After completing the graph, I was able to go back and think about his life. His father deserted him when he was three years old, and his mom was the closest thing to a witch that I have ever known. One time we had to stay with her while my mom was in the hospital. She would beat us, and the next day the neighbors would ask, "Are you girls okay?"

Once when I was thirteen, she beat me so bad in the back that I was in the hospital for two weeks and almost lost my kidney. Another thing his mom did was change the Bible records, so my dad could enter the Marines at the age of fifteen. No wonder my dad was empty and shallow! I could understand why he was the way he was. That didn't excuse him, because he could have learned better, but what this new awareness did was help me to realize that I wasn't defective, that there was nothing really wrong with me! What was defective was my relationship with my dad—and what *he* brought to our relationship. Understanding that was an incredible gift!

March 2007: Discover Dad Died

Because the Lord is requiring great transparency of me, I need to confess that over the years after Grief Recovery® helped me heal in so many ways, I felt vague promptings to call my dad. Since I'd acquired communication skills and was free of any bitterness and unforgiveness, a visit or talk seemed inevitable. But somehow, I kept putting it off, and my busy schedule was an unspoken excuse. It had been nineteen years since the visit with John where he'd ignored us.

On the morning of February 1, 2007, the Lord spoke to me during my quiet time in prayer. This is what He said:

Go to your father and pray a blessing over him, releasing any generational thing that needs to be released. It shall be a sign of putting to rest a relationship of pain—a relationship of hurts that was given by Me to prepare you for your calling.

This was your gift from Me. You recognized it, forgave when I showed you the way, and you have thanked Me many times, both in private and in public, for the gift of your parents. So now it is time to complete it and put it to rest, as the ending is here and a new day is beginning. For I am love, and you are My faithful daughter.

This shall be a gift of love to a dying man. And we will use it to show the world how we are to love one another.

When God told me to do this, I was shocked. Then I said, "All right, Lord, I'll do anything for You." A couple of weeks passed, and I experienced a stage of excitement. How was God going to use this to show His people how to love? Two more weeks went by, and I was still waiting. At that point it became real. I felt I had to move quickly.

On Saturday, March 31, I paid ten dollars through the Internet and found Dad's address and phone number. The next day at church, my pastor had an altar call. I've been a member of Chickamauga Presbyterian Church now for ten years, and they'd never had an altar call before. But here was our pastor, asking if anyone wanted prayer to come forward, so I did. I asked for the courage to make the call of reconciliation with my father.

I told a friend after church that I felt like the neat little package that I had my life all wrapped up in was being untied, that God was pulling off the strings, and was beginning to unwrap the package.

I planned to call between 2:00 and 3:00 on Sunday afternoon. I even checked the Internet again to see if Dad was listed in the Death Records before I made the call. About five years before, I'd called an old phone number to see if it was still his number. I wasn't expecting him to answer, and when he did, I was unprepared and caught off guard. I didn't know what to say. I hadn't planned that part. So I hung up.

To avoid that scenario, I prepared a speech and wrote it out. I took a deep breath, dialed the number with my prepared speech in front of me, and his wife answered the phone. I asked to speak to Kenny, and she said he wasn't there. She asked me who was calling, and I told her.

"Oh, Nancy, I'm so sorry—your dad died September 15th, and I had no way to get in touch with you." She paused, and added, "I've played this moment over and over in my mind, that you would call, and it would be too late." She told me that Dad was buried in his dress blues at the National Cemetery in Quantico. He got sick in 1995 with lung cancer, and after treatments, he went into remission. But in August of 2006, he discovered it was back. He died three weeks later of a heart attack. She told me that she'd said to him several times, "You need to call Nancy," but his reply was always, "Why? She doesn't care anything about me."

I told her of the times I'd sent cards to his post office box. Each card had a return address if he'd wanted to make contact. She said he'd never told her about them, that he was always the one who went to the post office; she never did. Every morning he would go check the mail, and then have coffee with the guys. "You know, Nancy, your dad was such a private person. I was married to him for forty years, and I didn't know hardly anything about him," she said.

There was one question burning in my mind. "Did he ever get saved?" I asked. She said yes, and explained that after they'd moved back to Virginia, a place he hated, that one day he announced that if she would move back to North Carolina with him, he'd go to church. She said he went every Sunday with her. Sometime before he died, she asked him if he was OK with Jesus, and he said yes.

We talked for a few more minutes, and I asked if she had a picture of him that she could send me, so I'd have something to show my grandchildren. She said she had two, one when he was young, and one in his dress blues, and she would put them in the mail the next day. She asked me what was happening in my life, and I filled her in. She said,

"Your dad would've been so proud of you."

When I hung up, my husband asked me who I'd been talking with on the phone. I told him that I'd just found out that my dad had died. Immediately, he began, "I told you that you should've called him. . ." I told him I didn't want to talk about it and went into my office (that's attached to our house). I grabbed a box of Kleenex and proceeded to cry. When my husband came to check on me, I told him, "I'm going to cry, and I'll cry until I'm ready to stop, and I don't know how long that will be."

I was perfectly OK with not talking to or seeing my dad all the years after I did Grief Recovery®. I didn't feel a need to go to the "dry well" yet again. But when God told me to do this, I guess I was expecting a glory story. I was disappointed and hurt.

To do the work I do, the Lord requires the highest level of honesty from me. I might not always be comfortable with that level of transparency, but I do it because He wants my heart wide open. Finding out about my dad's death was like having a part of me unwrapped. I felt so incredibly sad. Sad that my dad died a broken and lonely man who believed he wasn't loved by his daughter. Sad that Dad had never been relieved of the guilt and regrets of his past. Sad that I'd missed God's gentle promptings to call over the past two years. Sad that I'd never attempted to communicate with him once I learned how. And, finally, I was sad that I no longer had a chance to practice God's amazing love by praying a blessing over him.

God's message to me on the first of February

was His heart on the matter. It was how He wanted the relationship to be resolved. I sat with His words on my lap, knowing that my waiting had cost me my Heavenly Father's perfect will from being accomplished. I cried for three days, and pushed myself to find a voice for every feeling that rose up in me. I examined each feeling in the moment I experienced it. I live by what I teach, believe me. This processing of your feelings in the moment you have them allows you to move on much more quickly.

I can't even begin to tell you how emotionally distraught I would have been if I hadn't completed my recovery work on my dad well before he died. I would've been left with my heart crunched, left with a million regrets and "what ifs." I think I would've been non-functional for a good period of time. Thank You, God, for Grief Recovery®!

Because of what I've done and know, I was able to work through all that sadness and pain in five days. And what were other people's reactions to my loss? My husband sent out an e-mail prayer chain, asking our church family to remember me in prayer. Well, one person came to my house and let me talk. Another spoke to me before our Wednesday night prayer meeting and asked if I was OK. During prayer that night, this same person prayed that God would be with me in my time of grief. That's it. No one else ever mentioned it. When the prayer meeting was over, no one said a word, not even my pastor! It's never been mentioned. There were no hugs, and we're a very hugging church. Most things our church does very well. If I'm sick with a cold or the flu, I receive cards from many people; but my dad dies, and I don't even get an "I'm sorry" or a hug.

These are the emotions I processed the week after I learned of my dad's death:

1. I'm sad that I don't have a glory story of restoration to share.
2. I'm sad that my dad died a broken man.
3. I know my dad loved me. God has reminded me of certain memories that affirm that, but because of the baggage my dad brought to the relationship, he couldn't press through it to reach out. He carried his burdens inside: a closed and lonely man.
4. I have to forgive my step-mother for the past.
5. I can see now how a lack of ability to communicate robbed a father and a daughter of their relationship.
6. Somehow I have to help people see the importance of working through the baggage and reaching out, in spite of the cloudy history within a relationship. When we age and the years seem numbered, there is a sense of "putting things to bed," and the righteous banners we carried in our youth don't seem so important anymore. Peace and reconciliation seem the right actions to take.
7. I wonder how blessing and reconciliation would've impacted my dad. Maybe those things we have to work through as we near death wouldn't have been so difficult and lonely for him.

Interestingly, in my grief, I didn't want the noise of my worship music. I wanted the guidance and calmness of God's Word. I wanted to be in His presence, to feel that peace that comes from resting in Him. Every moment, I knew that He was right at my side. It was very comforting, knowing that I wasn't going to fall off into an abyss, and was instead secured to the One who created everything.

The timing of this event, in the midst of finishing this book, I believe, was God's way of using a sad event for His glory.

CHAPTER 12
THE IMPORTANCE OF COMPLETION

After decades in the field of healing and recovery, I'm convinced that it is essential that we complete what is unfinished for us in regards to events we consider losses. The authors of *The Grief Recovery Handbook* remind us, "Incompleteness is not limited to major events. It is an accumulation of undelivered communications, large and small that have emotional value to you."[63] Remember: You don't have a broken head, but a broken heart. "Sometimes incompleteness is caused by our actions or non-actions. Other times it is caused by circumstances outside of our control."[64]

> Incompleteness has to do with things that, . . . we wish had ended different, better or more. We rarely ever know which interaction will be our last. It is not abnormal in many of our relationships to table a few topics that we plan to deal with later. This is not

necessarily procrastination, just a plan for later. But following a death or a divorce, such postponements often are some of the ingredients of incompleteness."[65]

We often have difficult relationships with living people—parents, siblings, others—where we wish things had been different or better. All too frequently, it's the accumulation of undelivered communications that limits us in these relationships as well. I think this is a very important statement. Most of us never come to the realization that undelivered communication from past relationships continues to impact us and limit us in present relationships. There are many reasons why there might be undelivered emotional communication:

- Others often won't listen to what we want to say.
- Sometimes we get sidetracked with other relationships, jobs, etc.
- Sometimes we forget to call or make time for that relationship.
- Sometimes the right time never comes.

Still, we end up stuck with undelivered emotional communication. In short, emotional incompleteness is any undelivered emotional communication. Please hear this: "Being emotionally incomplete does not mean that you are bad. It does not mean that you are defective. It only means that a variety of circumstances and actions or non-actions have robbed you of the opportunity to be complete."[66]

Is completion a Biblical idea? According to Paul,

"We proclaim Him, admonishing every man and teaching every man with all wisdom, so that we may present every man complete in Christ."[67] The word "complete" is the Greek word *teleios*. This word has caused much misunderstanding because of its unfortunate translation in the KJV, where it is translated "perfect." The meaning of the word is: "having reached its end, i.e. complete" (*NASB Greek & Hebrew Dictionary* [Updated Edition]). So, the word can mean that someone or something is perfect in having reached its end or its completion. When used of people, a better translation is probably "mature," and it is translated accordingly in a number of verses.

The verse reveals that Paul wanted to present the Colossians as "complete," having reached their designated end, or maturity in Christ. I like this concept, and it's very much related to completing the pain in our loss events, so that we might reach the end that God intended for us. Is that end maturity in Christ? I believe it is!

Paul not only talked about presenting every believer as complete in Christ, but he gave some of his ways of doing this, which included preaching Christ, admonishing and confronting every believer, and teaching every believer with all wisdom. Paul's goal and a major Grief Recovery® goal are very much compatible. The goal is that the believer, having completed the pain (and also having repented for the sin) in their relationships, might fully mature as a rightful heir in the Kingdom of God.

Now please keep in mind that if we had handled (and continue to handle) sins and loss events with immediate apologies, forgiveness, and significant emotional statements, there would be no need for Loss History Graphs, Relationship Graphs, and Completion Letters, except to clean up those things that we missed. In Christian language, this is called "keeping short accounts with God." But these tools now allow us to resolve or complete the pain of things that we didn't handle face-to-face.

According to the authors of *The Grief Recovery Handbook*, what we are completing is our relationship to the pain caused by the loss. We are completing anything that was left unfinished at the time of the loss. The only thing that can stop you is the fear that you'll forget your loved one. That is not possible.[68] You can't forget your loved one. Your physical relationship with your loved one may be over, but the emotional and psychological relationship continues on. What will be forgotten is the pain that has marred the memories of your loved one.

Completing Pain in Past Relationships Opens Our Hearts to New Ones

We get our hearts back by completing the pain in past relationships. "Completing earlier relationships makes one's heart open to new ones. Being open means that painful things hurt again, but it is that same hurt that allows us to be more loving. We are now open to the normal and healthy reactions to loss."[69] So, I'm sorry to tell you that you successfully completing the Grief Recovery® will not end your sadness; it will complete your pain. Please understand this! Sadness is a perfectly normal residue. As a matter of fact, Grief Recovery® allows one to have the normal feelings of sadness back as well as the good memories that were conflicted with pain.

Grief Recovery® can be likened to physical healing. If you've ever hurt or cut yourself physically, there can be a lingering effect if the injury is severe. After that spot is healed, bumping or pressing against that spot can still produce pain.

Successfully completing Grief Recovery® work will not only open our hearts to new relationships, it will allow us to be current or fully present in all of our relationships. When we sin or have incomplete loss events, they interrupt our fellowship with God, other people, and even ourselves. If we handle these sins or loss events through amends (apologies or repentance), forgiveness, and significant emotional statements to God and all other appropriate people, we'll stay current or fully present in those relationships. For us, God is a God of the here and now! He's the great "I AM!"

CHAPTER 13
RECOVERY COMPONENTS
FORGIVENESS AND AMENDS

There are three areas in which communication can be incomplete. The first is amends or apologies which encompass all the things for which you would need to apologize. These are the mistakes that you are responsible for whether intentionally or inadvertently within the context of the relationship.

The second area is that of forgiveness and includes all the offenses for which you might need to forgive the other person. This area includes things that did or did not happen from *your* perception. "When you forgive someone, you are dancing to the rhythm of the divine heartbeat. God invented forgiveness as the only way to keep his romance with the human race alive."[70]

Forgiveness can often be misunderstood when people equate it with condoning certain behavior. According to *Merriam-Webster's Collegiate*

Dictionary, to forgive means to "cease to feel resentment against (an offender)" whereas condone means "to treat as if trivial, harmless, or of no importance."[71]

The Grief Recovery® definition for forgiveness is "giving up the hope of a different or better yesterday." It's in the context of "hoping" that things can be different, better, or more that many emotions reside. I've found that using this definition helps clients to be able to move into the forgiveness area more easily.

If we're trying to recapture yesterday, holding on to how we want the story to be, or if we imagine different or better endings, then these vain imaginations hold our hearts captive. We can become obsessed with them. They hold us captive to yesterday, and they become the treasure that we are constantly seeking. Remember these words, "Where your treasure is, there your heart will be also."[72] Therefore, our hearts are with our treasures of hopes, dreams, or expectations of yesterday, trying to make them happen today.

Imagine a man standing in a jail cell with his right hand holding onto the bar on his right side (which represents the past) with a white clenched fist. Now, imagine his left hand holding onto the bar on his left side (which represents the future). All the while this is happening, there is no door or additional bars around this man that could possibly prevent him from walking out of the jail cell. As long as we refuse to forgive or let go of resentments, bitterness, disappointments, or expectations, we will remain in a prison of our own making.

The law of cause and effect needs to be

examined here. Let's illustrate this idea by using the case of a small child who's been sexually abused. The child is zero percent guilty in causing that abuse. However, it's probably affecting his/her life at one hundred percent. We all understand that we can't change what has happened to us in the past, even though we live our lives as if we could. So then what must happen for this child to be freed from the prison of the past? It will require a desire to begin and a willingness to take one-percent responsibility for how he or she is going to choose to respond to that event *today*. In taking that step, it doesn't condone or trivialize what has happened in the past. Nor does it negate the impact the event has had on his or her life. It's an action that will begin the process of setting that individual free.

It is tragic enough that bad things happen to us, but it's even more tragic that we allow those individuals to continue to control us, especially from the grave! When I refuse to forgive, it's like I have swallowed a glass of poison, and I'm expecting the other person to become sick! That's obviously not going to happen. Forgiving is making a choice to be free. Otherwise, the individual remains a victim stuck in jail.

Unfortunately, some people will choose to remain a victim because it earns them the attention they are craving, but others, when given a clear step-by-step path like Grief Recovery®, will apply the skills and walk out free, as Jesus' sacrifice has called us to be.

An important concept within Grief Recovery's definition for forgiveness is "hope." Now, the Bible encourages us to have hope, but that hope comes from knowing truth, Jesus Christ. What Grief Recovery® trainers too often see in grievers is a (false) hope that keeps people stuck--hoping that someday they can change yesterday, that someday Dad will be what he should've been, or that someday the relationship will be what it should've been. Even though all of us know intellectually that we can't change yesterday, so many of us keep repeating the same behaviors over and over, hoping they'll have a different outcome. Here's a picture of what that looks like.

Imagine that you're in the middle of the Sahara Desert, and it hasn't rained in five hundred years, and you just heard on the weather report that it's not going to rain for another five hundred years. You walk out in the middle of this desert until you find a well. You drop your bucket down, wait a few moments, and then draw it up. You look in the bucket and exclaim, "Darn, no water!" like it is some surprise. The next day you go to the same dry well and put the bucket down and are surprised when again it comes up empty. You need to understand that if there isn't any water in the well, you're not going to get any water out! We often expect people to have the same information in their brain box as we do, and then we're sorely disappointed when they don't.

Because others so often don't see things the way we do, forgiveness is a huge key for the whole process. If we hold on to unforgiveness, it becomes a stronghold for bitterness, anger, and all kinds of unhealthy emotions that Satan uses to keep us defeated. Forgiveness is a spiritual action. It's not about the other person; it's about you helping yourself. In addition, the act of forgiveness releases grace to someone else.[73]

The spiritual act of impartation to another allows you to receive more of what you've given out. That's why you don't become depleted; you actually receive more. So if the act of forgiving is impartation of grace to another, then think how much more grace we receive when we forgive.

We're taught in church to "forgive and forget." This takes the scriptural admonition to "forgive as Christ forgave us," and tacks onto it the requirement to forget, as well. We're never told that Christ forgot what had been done to him, only that he forgave the people who did it. Then when we forgive, but we can't forget, we feel guilty. The problem is forgiveness and forgetting are not equal.

As humans, unless our brains are damaged, impaired in some way, or God took His eraser to our minds and hearts, we don't have the capacity to forget major events in our lives. For example, think about the people who survived the Holocaust. Some of them have been able to forgive their perpetrators, haven't they? But do you think there's any way they could ever forget what happened to them? Absolutely not! When we forgive, it allows us to let go so the memories don't limit us from pursuing the present. The ability to remember is important. It helps us not to repeat hurtful behaviors.

Scripture references to forgiveness deal with God's forgiveness of our sins, and our need to forgive others. Jesus wants believers to take their responsibility in reconciling with any person who has something against them. Because our God is a God of forgiveness, once we repent, we also need to forgive ourselves! Let's look at how King David took ownership of his behavior, but how he appropriated God's forgiveness, so he wouldn't forsake his calling.

When Nathan rebukes David for murder and adultery, David confessed his sins against the Lord and repented. Despite the consequences of these sins, David was able to move beyond his guilt, reestablish his relationship with God, and reenter into a pure worship of his Creator. The unveiling of what he'd done and the release of the anguish in his soul allowed him to again hear the voice of God so that he could fulfill his destiny.[75]

Just as David did, we, too, need to take ownership for our behavior, to own what is ours. We should apologize for what we've done. Whether or not the other person forgives us is beyond our control. When you ask for forgiveness, make sure you're not trying to skip over the apology. In fact, don't ask for forgiveness. Make an apology. It's up to the other person to offer forgiveness. That's between that person and God.

Writing down things that we need to forgive someone for is an action that helps us to recall and tell the emotional truth about certain events in a relationship. Down the road, after we have dealt with all of human relationships, we may also need to forgive God, if we're going to overcome the disappointment that keeps us from being intimate with Him. We aren't forgiving God because He's done anything wrong, but because we *feel* that He has done something wrong in not fulfilling our hopes, dreams, and expectations—whether they're biblical or not.

Apologies and amends are tools of deep

repentance. Paul touched on this idea. "If possible, so far as it depends on you, be at peace with all men.[75] Peace is *not* always in our hands! We can apologize, and people can still choose not to forgive us! That is no longer our problem! This doesn't mean that we won't be sad or disappointed, but since we can't control other people, we needn't let their decisions ruin our lives.

Additionally, from a biblical perspective, we should also make amends where possible. We should seek to undo what we have done when that is possible. Sometimes it is *not* possible! We can't undo murder, adultery, or broken trust. We can undo thievery, some lies, insensitive behavior, and judgments.

Let's look at the apology or repentance of David to God, regarding his sin with Bathsheba.

Be gracious to me, O God, according to Your loving kindness; according to the greatness of Your compassion blot out my transgressions. Wash me thoroughly from my iniquity and cleanse me from my sin. For I know my transgressions, and my sin is ever before me. Against You, You only, I have sinned and done what is evil in Your sight, so that you are justified when You speak and blameless when You judge. Behold, I was brought forth in iniquity, and in sin my mother conceived me.[76]

How does God respond to such confessions of repentance? "The sacrifices of God are a broken spirit; a broken and a contrite heart, O God, You will not despise."[77] In other words, it's our brokenness over our deep understanding of our sins that makes our confession to God acceptable. But how can we be acceptably broken or deeply cognizant of our sins if we do not allow God to search the secret rooms of our heart?

.

CHAPTER 14
GRIEF RECOVERY ACTION STEP 3
THE COMPLETION LETTER

We've already looked at how God made significant emotional statements when Adam and Eve fell in the Garden of Eden. Significant emotional statements help us to complete communication that is incomplete. This action allows us to become aware of those things that we wished we had said, when the person was alive, married to us, or when we were on better terms.

There's nothing new about writing a letter to a person. The Grief Recovery® Completion Letter is the most thorough, yet concise, method I've seen in my twelve years of practice, for organizing and expressing the emotional truth of our relationships. John James, the founder of The Grief Recovery Institute, developed this method almost thirty years ago, and in my opinion, it's still the most effective method available.

James suggests that you use your Relationship Graph, your list of amends, forgives, and significant emotional statements as a guide to help as you begin to write your letter. The letter is to be a free- flowing narrative that includes what you've discovered. However, the order of significant emotional statements is very important. As you begin, always express the amends first, so that you're taking accountability for your behavior or lack of behavior in the context of the relationship. Secondly, cover the areas in which you need to forgive the other person. Those will be all the areas that they're responsible for—things they have done or not done—within the context of the relationship. And finally, include all the significant emotional statements left in your heart.

Because the letter is a free-flowing narrative, some of the significant emotional statements may be mixed up in the context of the amends and forgive sections, and that's fine. But just remember to state your forgiveness before you add a significant emotional statement relating to it; otherwise, you will negate the impact that event had on you. One final instruction is to end your letter with a good-bye. When you write, "good-bye," you're not saying goodbye to the relationship, but to the pain and incompleteness of the relationship. A "good-bye" tells your brain that the work has been completed.

The point of the letter is to take away the pain, any unfinished business, and all the unmet dreams, expectations, and hopes you might have had for that relationship. It doesn't mean you won't be sad from time to time. Sadness is normal. But there's a huge difference between sadness and pain. Pain can be paralyzing, as we've discussed; but sadness, without pain, doesn't hinder us from fully embracing our present lives.

Below is my first Grief Recovery ® Completion Letter written to my dad in January of 1996:

Dear Dad,

I've been reviewing our relationship, and I've discovered some things that I want to say.

Dad, first I want to apologize for the part I played in our incomplete relationship. I judged you so harshly for the lack of communication, the un-connectedness, and the lack of physical touch (which would have given me the feeling of being alive and loved). I inadvertently failed to communicate with you as well, by not telling you how I felt or what was going on. The silence you taught me I learned well and have used throughout my life to build my false wall of protection from the pain of feeling.

Daddy, when you never touched me or held me or told me you loved me, in my child heart I believed I must be defective. Surely, if I wasn't defective, you would've loved me. As a result of my strong overpowering desire to have your approval and love, to have that connectedness, my life has been profoundly affected, especially my own ability to have and maintain relationships.

Dad, I forgive you for robbing me of the love and acceptance every little girl deserves from her Daddy, for the loss of my childhood and the loss of the ability to let a man into the inner part of my heart. I forgive you for the loss of dreams I had of a family, love, and completeness.

Dad, I want very much to tell you that I now see you as a broken little boy in a man's body with no skills to restore your heart. So how could you have taught me how to explore and restore my heart?

Dad, thank you for the times in my life you tried, like when you took me for a ride to get an ice cream, and you let me sit in your lap and steer the car. That is the happiest memory I have of my childhood. Thank you, Dad, for giving me that memory. And the time you let me hold your hand in the airport. You didn't pull away, and I realize now how much we both enjoyed those few moments.

Dad, I have loved you all my life, but for many years I've hated what I felt you robbed me of.

Dad, today I'm saying goodbye to all the pain associated with my childhood beliefs and goodbye to the incomplete picture I've carried all these years. I'm saying good-bye to the person I have been as a result of my pain.

Thank you, Dad, for giving me the positive times. These lost, but now found, memories have allowed me to find the courage to tell you how I feel and share my soul with you for the first time in my life. I wish we had more time, but I want you to know how much I truly love you just the way you are.

Goodbye Daddy, I'll miss you.

Your daughter,

Nancy

The final step in Grief Recovery® involves the action of reading the letter to a certified Grief Recovery® trainer or another person who understands the principles of sharing and is a safe, encouraging presence. Knowing that another person actually heard the words tells our brain that the information was delivered. It's a very powerful experience, maybe because it lines up with the biblical principle of confessing our sins to one another so that we may be healed.[78]

I have witnessed clients forgive and be able to love their parents after having experienced horrid injustices. I 'm reminded of Mary, now in her sixties, whose mother's live-in boyfriend sexually molested her from the age of three until she finally was able to leave home at eighteen. Her mother was aware of the actions, but allowed the behavior because she needed his money to feed her other four children and fill the emptiness in her own heart.

Mary had never spoken a word about the experience to anyone. She was able to follow the Grief Recovery® process and in so doing was able to forgive her mother and be set free from a lifetime of pain. The Completion Letter created room in Mary's heart, so she could feel love for her mother for the first time.

Keeping Current: Post Script

Now that the relationship has been emotionally completed, it's important to keep it current. That means from time to time new memories may come to the surface, and as they arise, it's important to complete them as well. This can be done in the form of a simple post script at the end of your already-completed letter. Following the same outline, you'd include the amends, forgives, and significant emotional statements as they apply to your new awareness. You would then follow through, and read the P.S. letter to another person.

Months before to finding out he'd died, I was prompted by the Holy Spirit to go to my father and pray a blessing over him. At first, I was stunned, but then excitement set in as I imagined that I might have the chance to pray over my now elderly father and let him be at peace about our relationship. After having completed my relationship graph and completion letter, I was free for the first time in my life to be able to communicate to my dad what was in my heart. Sadly, I delayed in answering this prompting. Below is my recent post script letter to my dad as an example.

* * *

April 1, 2007

P.S. Dad,

Well, it has been a long time since our last conversation, and I've discovered some things that I want to share with you:

Dad, I apologize for never contacting you after I learned communication skills. I knew that you didn't have them, and I could've taken the steps to try to make peace with you. As believers we are called to reconciliation because of the incredible love God showed us. As I process my grief, I'm learning new things each day. A special blessing the Lord has given me are memories that I had lost which reinforce the fact that you really did love me.

Once I did my grief recovery work on you in January of 1996, I was emotionally complete. I was at peace and finally gave up the hope that you would someday be what I wanted you to be. I let it be okay that you are who you are and that you didn't have the ability or skills to give me what I needed. It was the first time I realized that what you brought to the relationship from your childhood and past preempted your ability to be a communicating father.

Dad, I forgive you for not contacting me and letting me know that you were sick. Dad, I forgive you for never telling me that you became a believer. Dad, I forgive you for not telling Louise that I had sent you cards and for telling her that I didn't care anything about you.

Dad, I want you to know that the knowledge of your death has brought me great sadness. Sadness that you died not believing I loved you when I have loved you since the day I was born. Sadness that you missed so much of my life--that you never knew your grandson. We've both turned out to be committed Christians and strive to make a difference in the world. It's sad that we never got to talk about your new-found faith.

Dad, I don't know what will happen tomorrow. I don't know what else God will show me in all of this, but I do know that what happened to us will be shared with the world in an attempt to prevent this from happening to others.

I have thanked God many times for the parents that He chose to give me because without you and Mom and our experiences together (the good and the bad), I would not have been prepared to fulfill my life's calling. So Dad, don't worry about regrets. You were part of what God had planned for me. And I could not have been all that I am without your influence in my life. Dad, I've shared our story (my Relationship Graph) with thousands of people over the past ten years, and countless numbers of people have received the courage to press in and do their healing work. So, our relationship has been a winner in the end because you've shaped my life in such a way that the world is a better place because of our relationship. Now that you are in heaven, I'm sure that you understand that miracle, and probably you understand the depths of it all more than even I can comprehend.

Rest in peace now, Dad, knowing that our generational curse of non-communication has finally been broken, and God is receiving the glory.

I love you so,

Nancy

As I've worked with many Christians over the years, I saw a need for some of them to add an additional piece at the end of their Grief Recovery ® work. The power of the process often results in emotional communication that needs to be delivered to God. In the freeing of the heart, the flood of God's love pours in and whatever particular experience occurs needs to be communicated to Him. So, I suggest that clients write a prayer to God, so they are complete with Him as well. The prayer is a free-flowing expression of their love and gratitude for this new place in their heart God has opened up. There's no right or wrong way to do it. Just allow the Holy Spirit to flow through you as you write it down.

Below is an example of my prayer I wrote following my P.S. letter to my father.

* * *

Father God, thank You for all that You are teaching me.

Thank You again for my dad and how he shaped my life. Thank You for having such wisdom and impeccable timing. To give me this lesson at this moment in my journey is really profound.

You became my Daddy in 1960, and You are the lover of my soul. Nothing on this earth holds a candlestick to the peace and love You shower me with. I want to complete the assignments that You've given me with the highest of honor that blesses Your name.

I look forward to that future day that You've appointed when I can go home to be with You where I belong. Funny, I realized today that since You adopted me into Your family, I have never doubted my place as Your daughter. What an incredible blessing!

Love,

Nancy.

CHAPTER 15
USELESS FIRES ON MY ALTAR

On February 15, 2007, God led me to the first chapter of Malachi. As I read about the defiled, diseased, and crippled animals that were put on the altar to sacrifice to Him, God began to speak to me about today's Church. These are His words; I wrote them down just as a secretary takes dictation:

It is an abomination to me. Today you do not sacrifice animals, but you bring to me your limited time, all the while looking to see if the time has passed so you can be finished. You continually wander off on all the things of this world. You don't take the time to clear out the clutter of the world, nor do you take the time to wait on me. You rush through and never give thought to ask what I want you to pray. You act like prayer is about you. It is not. It is about

Me. You see, everything is about Me. I am the Creator. You are the created. Have you forgotten?

You say, "What a burden!" The load is heavy when you carry dead animals (works). If your activities/sacrifices were from a pure, transparent heart, your load would not be a load. It would be a byproduct of a clean transparent heart, a byproduct of trust and love. What has happened to My people? They have gone way down the road, having passed Me by in their zealous quest that is driven and motivated by their own "self-agendas" or "what they think I want." They never stop to ask Me; they just assume. How arrogant and prideful. Where is the humility?

I am your strength and defender. Since when were you to go out in your own power? I never gave you permission to do that.

Then God brought my eyes to Malachi 2:5. He continued,

My covenant with Levi "was a covenant of life and peace, and I gave them to him; this called for reverence and he revered Me and stood in awe of My name."[79] Where is your reverence? Where is your awe?

Then, at the Lord's prompting, my eyes rested on these words, "True instruction was in his (Levi's) mouth and nothing false was found on his lips."[80]

God continued,

> Your false instruction is teaching My people to live in their heads, to pride themselves in their intellectual knowledge of Me and My Word. You are the hands of Satan, leading my children away from their hearts. You teach false doctrines, false instruction, while saying, "Thus saith the Lord." How disgusting your self-righteous piety and false teachings are to Me. My children need to hear My heart. I didn't ask for their intellect. I ask for their heart on a daily basis. Levi listened for My heart, for My instructions. He did not go out in his own power and wisdom. He listened for My instructions. He didn't make assumptions based on his intellect/reason. He walked with Me in peace and uprightness and turned many away from sin.[81]

These are bold and powerful words; but we serve a bold and powerful God. Tragically, many believers are confounded by the events in their lives. "Where is God in all of this?" they want to know. Nothing has changed in what true believers in the One True God are supposed to do. They are supposed to *diligently seek God on a daily basis*, and now that we have the Holy Spirit dwelling within us instead of just landing upon us as in Ezekiel's day, we can *abide* in God as Jesus asked us to do in order to accomplish his perfect will.

The Bible makes it clear that we do not receive because we do not ask. Since God already knows our material needs, what He's referring to is our asking for spiritual guidance and gifts. We must ask for these because He will not foist upon us the keys to His Kingdom. Here's an example of one of my personal prayers to God. It's not included as a model for you to copy, but as a statement so you can have a glimpse of my heart and know that God wants to share spiritual truth with all those who diligently seek Him.

Father God,

You sent me hope. Hope is a new picture, a deeper level to press into so that I can draw closer to You. Increase my discernment, so that I can help Your Church and complete the task that You've given me.

I want more of you Lord! Whenever I get down, it's always because I need more of You. I need to draw closer. Closer is never enough. I want ALL of YOU. Take me there, Father, whatever that picture looks like. Take my hands, Lord, for Your service. Take my ears, Lord, for Your service. Take my eyes, Lord, that I might see based on Your ascension. Take my nose that I might smell Your sweet fragrance. Take my senses that I might feel the heat of Your presence.

I pray that Your presence might engulf me Father, so that You, O God, might be glorified--so that I would be so full and overflowing with Your Holy Spirit that the atmosphere in the room would change when I enter, wearing Your reflection.

In Yeshua's holy name! Amen!

CHAPTER 16
IF YOU DILIGENTLY SEE ME

When I read the words the Lord poured out to me on February 15th, I'm reminded that we're living in a time of great blessings and a time of judgment—and judgment, as we know, comes to the Church first because the unsaved are meant to know us by our love for one another.

Way too many people try to love one another in their own strength. That's not God's love coming through us; that's a pale, meager, pruned kind of love. That's the tragedy in the church today. The world is not transformed by our love because it's not a true reflection of God's immense, overwhelming, healing, and transformative love.

If we're willing to seek the Lord with all our heart, He will heal us and cleanse us from whatever is keeping us from His love, from fulfilling our life's calling (what He created us to do). We don't "seek God with all our heart" by going to church, though that can be part of it. We don't diligently seek God by attending Bible studies, though that can be a facet. We don't diligently seek God by keeping a tidy set of rules. We seek God with all our hearts by being still in His presence, going off to be alone with Him as Jesus did, by guarding our time with Him (and not rudely answering the phone in the midst of our devotions). Is that a radical notion to you, not answering the phone during your quiet time with the Lord? Well, it shouldn't be. If you could *see* the Creator of the Universe sitting beside you, wouldn't you do all you could to make Him feel honored and welcomed? Meet Him early each morning before you begin your day, before your children are clamoring for attention. Meet Him even in the dark morning hours as Jesus did, for an uninterrupted encounter. If you show up with expectation, He will meet you.

The people I know whose lives are guided by God on a daily, even moment-by-moment basis, treat our God as the King of Kings. They take that first commandment seriously, and when they sit down with Him, He clearly speaks to their spirit, and what they lay their hands to succeeds, because He has advised them in *every detail* about His Kingdom work.

Our culture is so much about *doing* and not about *being*. Being in God's presence changes you; after a while it makes you equipped, in a personal way, to do what you were created to do. There are no *shortcuts*, though there are *helps*, like Grief Recovery.

God has walked me through a life of much pain and turned it all into an orchard. People, even the most determined of us, *can't do that*, but God can, and He promises to do that if we diligently seek Him. Some people think they are diligent if they arrive at church for an early Sunday sermon. Some think they are diligent if they read several chapters of His book each day. Diligence is doing what God asks you to do. For one, it may be hospitality that day. For another, it might be helping a friend move. God is too big for formulas, and He will not be limited by one denomination's good ideas.

What has God asked you to do today? Yesterday? The day before? If you can't answer that question except by quoting Bible verses, you need to repent for not keeping the first commandment. Ask Him to put a desire in you to pursue Him with all your heart. Let's meditate on the following verses (all are NIV translations):

Proverbs 13:4: "The sluggard craves and gets nothing, but the desires of the diligent are fully satisfied." Proverbs 21:5:"The plans of the diligent lead to profit as surely as haste leads to poverty." John 5:39-40: "You diligently study the Scriptures because you think that by them you possess eternal life. These are the Scriptures that testify about me, yet you refuse to come to me to have life." John 5:42: "I know that you do not have the love of God in your hearts." The writer of Hebrews encourages his readers to be diligent in seeking God and His ways. Hebrews 6:11-12: "We want each of you to show this same diligence to the very end, in order to make your hope sure. We do not want you to become lazy, but to imitate those who through faith and patience inherit what has been promised." Deuteronomy 4:29: "But if from there you seek the Lord your God, you will find him if you look for him with all your heart and with all your soul." 1 Samuel 13:14: ". . . the Lord has sought out a man after His own heart and appointed him leader of his people. . . " I Chronicles 16:10: "Glory in his holy name; let the hearts of those who seek the Lord rejoice." I Chronicles 16:11: "Look to the Lord and his strength; seek his face always." 1 Chronicles 22:19: "Now devote your heart and soul to seeking the Lord your God."

Let's take these verses to heart! He called us to enjoy that intimate relationship that exists between a husband and wife, where two become as one. They glory in the aroma, the warmth, the energy that flows, as they become one flesh with no beginning and no end. But the greatest gift we can receive, but also give to the world, is our true, unhindered self living in loving union with God. How can we in the church affirm other people's unique identities if we don't affirm our own? No matter where you are on the relationship spectrum with God, He's calling us all to move closer and closer. One day during my time with the Lord, He led me to read in a daily devotional book by Sarah Young titled *Jesus Calling*.

I am calling you to a life of constant communication with Me. Basic training includes learning to live above your circumstances, even while interacting on that cluttered plane of life. You yearn for a simplified lifestyle, so that your communication with Me can be uninterrupted. But I challenge you to relinquish the fantasy of an uncluttered world. Accept each day just as it comes, and find Me in the midst of it all. Talk with Me about every aspect of your day, including your feelings. Remember that your ultimate goal is not to control or fix everything around you; it is to keep communing with Me. A successful day is one in which you have stayed in touch with Me, even if many things remain undone at the end of the day.

Do not let your to-do list (written or mental) become an idol directing your life. Instead, ask My Spirit to guide you moment by moment. He will keep you close to Me.[82]

Is our appraisal of how well we are doing based upon our limited, worldly frame of reference" and not on a heavenly perspective? What if we're all wrong?! What if the time alone with God and not the productivity is what will not burn up when we stand before Him, even if that productivity was good and necessary or even our ministry? What if we stand before Him and say, "But. . ." to explain our good works, and He replies, "But I was calling you to come visit Me and spend time with Me, and you ignored My heart crying out to you!" Oh my, how sad and heartbreaking it will be for us. How deeply it must grieve Him when we don't want to spend time with Him, when we turn our backs on our Lover.

CHAPTER 17
WHY LEADERS NEED TO DO GRIEF RECOVERY WORK

More and more Christian authors are advocating the kind of inner healing process embodied in some of our Grief Recovery® actions.

The work of growing in Christ (what theologians call sanctification) does not mean we don't go back to the past as we press ahead to what God has for us. It actually demands we go back in order to break free from unhealthy and destructive patterns that prevent us from loving ourselves and others as God designed.[83]

Larry Crabb makes the point that we need to revisit our theology on sanctification. We accept the part about what it takes to receive life from God, but do we really understand what's required of us to live the sanctified life once we have received it?"[84]

The sons of Korah wrote, "God is our refuge and strength, a *very present* help in time of trouble" (emphasis mine).[85] That's why we need to become fully present to tap into God's help! When we are unhealed, it's very difficult to be fully present. Too many church leaders are trying to minister to people without being fully present! That's why I'm asking all leaders to do this grief work. When we recover our hearts, we will not only be complete, mature, open to new relationships, and fully present in our relationships, we will be healthy.

Here is a powerful definition of healthy, mature self-love: having the willingness and ability to allow yourself the right to make your own choices for yourself, without the need of approval from others. We all desire affirmation and approval from people who are significant to us, but that's quite different than needing the approval of others. The opposite of self-love is self-rejection, and one of the symptoms of self-rejection is that negatives adhere to us, while positives and affirmations seem to bounce off.

A healthy love for others includes the willingness and ability to allow others the right to make their own choices for themselves without any insistence that they satisfy us. Many of us are trying to get something out of people that we love, and it blocks our willingness and ability to let them make their own choices. If people love us with a healthy, mature, Spirit-led love, their love for us will be wonderful and touch us deeply. If they don't love us with a healthy, mature, Spirit-led love, our insistence that they satisfy us will still not facilitate a love that will deeply touch us.

So many of us are working towards and praying

for a great healing to take place in the church. Currently, there's a communal lack of healing that's impacting our ability to relate in a healthy way to relatives, to others in our "family of God," and to pre-Christians to whom we might be ministering. This inability to reflect God's perfect love to others needs to change.

Researchers have been collecting data and studying why such large numbers of men and women who profess a genuine commitment to Christ are leaving the church ("church leavers"). Their research revealed three main reasons for leaving:

> 1 Those who no longer attend church saw "the same emotional conflicts inside the church as outside."

> 2 Those who become inactive (they internally checked out) "realized the black and white presentations of the life of faith did not fit their life experiences."

> 3 Those who left their faith completely "grew weary of Christians who regardless of their 'knowledge' of God, church involvement, and zeal, were angry, compulsive, highly opinionated, defensive, proud, and too busy to love the Jesus they professed."[86]

Sadly, church-goers do not look much different from those who are un-churched, according to Gallup polls and sociologists.

- Church members divorce their spouses as often as their secular neighbors.

- Church members beat their wives as often as

their neighbors.

- Church members' giving patterns indicate they are almost as materialistic as non-Christians.

- White evangelicals are the most likely people to object to neighbors of another race.

- Of the "higher-commitment" evangelicals, 26 percent think premarital sex is acceptable, while 46 percent of "lower-commitment" evangelicals believe it to be okay also.[87]

Ron Sider, the author of *The Scandal of Evangelical Conscience,* writes, "Whether the issue is marriage and sexuality or money and care for the poor, evangelicals today are living scandalously unbiblical lives. . . . The data suggest that in many crucial areas evangelicals today are not living any differently from their unbelieving neighbors."[88] If we're going to be responsible for raising up the next generation of pastors and leaders, we must take these points about resolving emotional pain very seriously. "How can you enter someone else's world when you have not entered your own?"[89] You can't help others or disciple future leaders in areas where you aren't healed!

Choosing brokenness will set us free. It's the model that Christ presented in His life, and it's the model that we must follow as well. Discipleship must always begin with us. As we become broken, humble, and clean on a daily path, people will be drawn to us just as they were to Christ.

Here's an illustration of why we need resolution with our stuffed-down, or barely-hidden pain. If I have a glass of water that's almost full, and I try to pour more water into it, what do you suppose is going to happen? Not much of the intended new water is going to end up in the glass, and that which does get inside the glass will overflow or be so insubstantial that it's hardly noticeable. That's exactly the situation with the church today. We've focused so much on pouring Bible knowledge, rules, and regulations into a person that we've forgotten to help them resolve the past and move it up and out so there's room for the new. The new water (God's Word) is wonderful and important, but we have to make room for it, so it has a home to reside in. Our hearts have to be cleaned out, so there's room for God's precious Word, and we gain an ability to believe it within our hearts and not just in our heads.

Most of us rarely see genuinely authentic people, those who live and speak from their hearts. One exception is children. At first, they are transparent. When their loss-of-trust issues begin, they start closing down their hearts to protect themselves from additional pain. Could it be that's why Jesus admonished us to become as little children?

And what about the impact this lack of healing has on our image to unbelievers? Why would they want what we have? God called us to be joyful and free, and yet, it certainly appears that way too many of us are still in bondage. Bondage isn't a result of God's inability to set us free. However, as long as we're holding on to the past, we'll stay stuck in jail. We need help to let go and to get out. Think how it grieves God's heart to be offering us such wonderful and precious treasures that we can't embrace because our hands are full.

It's time for the church to wake up, take off their grave clothes, and walk out into the light. And it *must* begin with leaders setting the example.

.

CHAPTER 18
WE MUST ALLOW TIMES OF SORROW
(SO WE CAN REAP MORE JOY)

When I was coming to the end of *The Journey of Desire* by John Eldredge, I came across this paragraph,

> I believe we must add two spiritual disciplines to everyday life.

> The first is worship. We must adore God deliberately, regularly.

> The other is grief. We must allow a time of sorrow to do our own personal sowing. I see no other way to care for our hearts.[90]

After reading these words, the following truth broke upon me like a radiant sun breaking over the horizon and into my room on an expectant spring morning: The Grief Recovery® Program is a tool, a very excellent tool, but alas, still a tool.

Incredibly, grief itself is a spiritual discipline that is put forth and described all through the Bible. It's experienced by Jesus Christ to procure our salvation, and modeled for our example (He was a man of sorrows and acquainted with grief). It was arranged by our Heavenly Father to cleanse and heal our hearts and woo us back to Himself (the Lord was pleased to crush Him, putting Him to grief). He will one day, in heaven, wipe away every loss, pain, sorrow, sadness, and grief. Until then, we must allow time for suffering, sorrow, and grief to do their perfect work. Is that what the psalmist realized when he prayed, "Restore our fortunes, Lord, as streams renew the desert. Those who plant in tears will harvest with shouts of joy. They weep as they go to plant their seed, but they sing as they return with the harvest."[91]

Sorrow is our sowing, and rejoicing is our reaping! As we continue to make time for personal times of sowing, we shall reap more and more joy. It's grief that will circumcise and prepare our hearts for true, living, intimate worship of God. It's grief that will allow us to be fully present enough to give all that we are in worship to God, because of all that He is. It's grief that will allow us to enter into passionate, unabashed, delicious, breathtaking intimacy with the Lover of our Souls, Jesus Christ!

As praise is a means of taking territory back from the devil, and worship is the means of ratifying the covenant promises of God, so grief is the means of recapturing and living through our hearts, so that praise and worship might be released unto their full potential.

Look for Him in the storms. That's where the treasure is: "I will give you the treasures of darkness, riches stored in secret places, so that you may know that I am the Lord, the God of Israel, who summons you by name"[92] The journey and search for Him in the midst of the darkness is what builds our faith and transforms us into more of His likeness. Searching for Him in the midst of the storm is where our power comes from. The development of the relationship comes from time spent with Him: questioning, lamenting, and claiming His Word, while holding tight to His promises amidst our questions, anger, fear, and depression.

.

CHAPTER 19
TESTIMONIES

Testimony #1

While attending the American Association of Christian Counselors International Conference in August of 2001, I met Pastor Glenn Murphy, a Family Life Pastor of a large church in New Jersey. I had a booth in the exhibit hall and was selling books and advertising the Grief Recovery® Certification Training. Pastor Murphy came by my booth four or five times during the course of the conference. He inquired about my doing a training class at his church.

Several weeks later, we all experienced the devastation of what happened at the World Trade Center. I immediately began praying, telling God He knew I had the skills to help. I asked Him to please open a door for me to be able to go. Two days later, I received a call from Pastor Murphy wanting to know how soon I could make it to his church to do a training class. His church is in Basken Ridge, New Jersey, and many people in that community worked at the World Trade

Centers.

Two weeks later I trained a class of fourteen from their church and community. A woman named Carol came in, and you could see the pain all around her. She explained that two years earlier, the man she was engaged to marry had died of cancer; then, a few months later, Carol's only child, who was four years old, also died of cancer. Her sister was critically injured in the Trade Center attacks, and her cousin was killed, and seven of her friends were missing. (They were never recovered.) All of these events had occurred in just two years' time. Understandably, Carol was really angry with God.

After the training was over, Carol wrote a note to me, saying, "I've cried more in the last four days than I ever have in my life, and for the first time, I feel like I've been set free." During our last session as a group, another woman confessed that when she'd walked in, and saw how Carol embodied so much pain, she felt afraid of her and had taken a seat across the room. Now, Carol looked like a different person.

None of these people had ever attended a grief recovery outreach program before and wouldn't have known if the program worked or not. Now they were able to see that no matter how horrific life's situations are, the program works. They had experienced the immediate beginning of healing that's available.

There would be more classes there in the future, but here are excerpts from the first letter I received from Pastor Murphy.

Words cannot begin to express the depth of my appreciation to you for the Grief Recovery® Certification Training you provided to our church. It has had a powerful impact upon me both personally and in the "soul care" work I do as a pastor and therapist. In addition, my fellow classmates from our church have confirmed to me that this training has been literally life-changing, for them, too. They have reported to me that they, "no longer see people the same way," "have learned how to listen," "are now able to recognize the unique language of a broken heart," "have personally resolved losses that have been adversely impacting their lives for years," and "have been equipped with the tools and skills needed to help people who carry broken hearts."

As you may recall, I was both deeply drawn to this kind of training and yet scared to participate in it. On some level I knew that this training was a "missing key" that I needed professionally and more importantly, personally, but I was afraid of what might be uncovered in my heart. Prior to attending the training I had dealt with most of my losses in life on a largely intellectual and spiritual level, but not on an emotional level. Through this training I came to discover that no amount of spiritual or intellectual truth can mend a broken heart. But thankfully, I am able to now report that my heart is mending in ways I never dreamed it needed to...or was capable of healing.

The most exciting part of all for me has been to see the impact that this training is having in my ministry and in the ministry effectiveness of the men and women of Millington Baptist Church who attended with me. I have seen "pew warmers" become active participants in the life of our church, and I have watched discouraged people become excited about using the tools and gifts they've discovered. These people have been released for ministry and are already making a difference in the lives of friends, neighbors, co-workers, and fellow church members.

Glenn T. Murphy M.A., LPC

Pastor of Family Ministries and Counseling

Millington Baptist Church

Basken Ridge, New Jersey

Testimony #2

As a pastor, counselor, and an individual, I wholeheartedly and enthusiastically support and recommend Sunrise At Midnight and the Grief Recovery Institute!

I signed up for this training as a way for our church and myself to better respond to the 9/11 Tragedy and a future bereavement ministry. I did not know what to expect other than increased knowledge.

Well, I did receive increased knowledge and skills, but somewhat surprisingly I received so much more as well! I discovered that I, and others, have far more significant loss issues in our lives than we ever realized. In addition, I came to the life-changing realization that many, if not most, of my struggles with frustration, my "buttons," rocky relationships, and how I interact with others is directly related to loss issues in my life.

Most encouraging and transforming of all, I came to understand and achieve actual recovery and resolution. And in the process, I learned the tools to continue to do this in my own life, while facilitating change and genuine healing in others as well!

Going through the Grief Recovery® Certification training has revolutionized my life, my family, my ministry, and my counseling. I do not make this claim lightly. And as I have begun our first Grief Recovery® Outreach Program in the church, I can see how it will also transform and energize not only the lives of the participants, but the church as well!

I entered this training to help those grieving the recent death of a loved one. In actuality, I am now effectively ministering to and facilitating recovery in individuals who have any of a wide variety of loss issues-- recent or past death, divorce, broken relationship, trust, personal violation, job loss, significant health problems, etc.

Todd G. Leupold

Pastor of Family Ministries

Brookdale Baptist Church

Bloomfield, New Jersey

Testimony #3

As a priest I know that the process of grieving, if handled wrongly, causes people to embrace life-destroying lies. These lies create seemingly unbreakable patterns that reveal themselves later in life as addictions, compulsions, perversions or other symptoms labeled "insanity." Unless the grief is resolved, science, psychology, and even religion offer no real hope.

In my own life, the process of Grief Recovery® as taught by the Grief Recovery Institute has opened my eyes to vast beds of submerged emotional pain that quietly hurt my life and ministry. Once these "raw spots" were exposed through the Grief Recovery® process, they could finally be healed by the grace of Jesus Christ.

Nancy's ministry has opened my eyes to the profound need in virtually every Christian community for an inner healing.

Fr. Chuck Huckaby

Priest, Law Enforcement Chaplain, and Youth Case Worker

Lawrenceburg, TN

Testimony #4

I praise God for your life and ministry . . . and for your love for people! What a treasure you have...of helping us see "The Real Jesus!" Thank you for your wonderful insight.

Rev. Lew Kimmel

Associate Pastor,

Dardena Presbyterian Church

Lake St. Louis, MO

Church Staffs

I knew that if I could work with the entire staff of a church, the healing experienced by these leaders would be modeled to their congregations. Members would see these men and women living from a place in their hearts.

One day I received another call from Pastor Murphy, and I listened as he shared his deep concern for the inability of his staff to work as a team any longer. Since making a corporate decision to find a vision for the church and have everyone work together for that goal as opposed to leaders doing their own thing, staff relationships began to decline. After some discussion, I offered to do a "Pastors' Retreat" for the church staff at Millington Baptist, which at that time had about 900 members. My only requirement was that I wouldn't be informing the participants of what would be involved in the retreat, and that they would have to be willing to step out on faith and trust that God would have His way.

I used the Grief Recovery® process to help them find the core issues, and it was amazing what happened as a result of that experience. The senior pastor shared with me that they had spent thousands of dollars attending classes at Princeton University, learning how to get a vision for their church. Yet, no matter what they tried, they couldn't seem to implement it. Then Peter, the Head Pastor, said, "But now for the first time, I have hope, and I know that we can do it." Pastor Glenn concluded that, "By addressing unresolved loss issues, we were able to once again function as a team instead of a collection of individuals."

At the time of the "Pastors' Retreat," the church had about 175 people who were a part of their ministry called the "Liquid Group" (which primarily focused on the twenty to forty year olds). Tim Lucas was their pastor. Several months after the retreat, Pastor Glenn called to report that, "Tim was standing in the pulpit preaching messages straight from his heart, and that people were coming from as far away as New York City to hear him." When I returned to the church nine months later, the "Liquid Group" numbers had risen to almost 600.

Below are the collective testimonies from the staff at Millington Baptist Church who attended the retreat. The pastors' testimonies have been ordered to capture their revelations on various topics. Participants included: Head Pastor, Peter Pendell; Worship Pastor, Mark Jones; Glenn Murphy, Family Life Pastor; Tim Lucas, Next Generation Pastor; and Al Riley, Pastor of Christian Education. The only participant not from Millington Baptist Church was Bill Brooks, Director of Counseling at Gateway Cathedral, in Staten Island, NY.

When I first thought about Grief Recovery®, I thought it was about those who had lost loved ones to death, but it is so much more than that. It is any sense in which you have an incomplete relationship with people present or past.

--Peter Pendall

Each of us, no matter who we are or what we do, if we have lived even a little bit of time in life or have had any type of relationship, there is going to come a time when people hurt us or a time when situations let us down. We are going to have to walk through some type of grief.

-- Mark Jones

One of the things that makes Grief Recovery® so very special, as far as I am concerned, is that it gets below the level of, "I'm fine; you're fine," and the answer, of course, that comes back is, "Sure, I'm fine, and everybody is fine," and really you know that we are not all fine, and that we are all broken people, and we have our own history of grief and difficulties to bear.

--Peter Pendall

Whether it is relationships or the loss of a relationship to death, whatever it might be, each of us is going to have some type of recovery that we are each going to need to have in our lives.

--Mark Jones

The Grief Recovery® program is unique in that it gives us a clear picture of how to think when we are thinking about our grief and emotions.

--Bill Brooks

The Grief Recovery® program offers a process

with steps that you can go through to actually regain your heart again.

--Glenn Murphy

Grief Recovery® provides the ability to deal with the broken relationships or incomplete relationships without necessarily going to those people but just going there in your own heart.

--Peter Pendall

It is really a crucial element for any person coming to maturity in Jesus Christ. They have to be able to deal with the past, but not only own their past baggage and sin, but actually deal honestly and come to a place of completion with people whom they have had difficult relationships with and have really never connected with on a heart level.

--Tim Lucas

Grief Recovery® training provided the skills and insight to be able to come up alongside people and give them a process to complete their loss.

--Bill Brooks

I found great value in it personally, because it allowed me to get in touch with some hidden emotions. And it really caused a spiritual awakening in my own heart and life.

--Al Riley

What I like about Grief Recovery® is that it really makes a head and a heart connection.

--Tim Lucas

We have a tendency to think with our heads and not with our hearts. The design of this course, it appears to me, really addresses the heart issues.

--Al Riley

Grief Recovery® really makes you roll up your sleeves, and do the hard emotional work.

--Tim Lucas

There just aren't any easy answers. We really had to address so many hard-core personal issues. Step one is there's value in self examination. Step two gives a solution of how to deal with these issues, and that I like as a practitioner.

--Al Riley

Grief Recovery® has really broken down barriers, especially in a group process.

--Bill Brooks

In fact, our church as a whole moved into this area of ministry and used it as an outreach, as well as an opportunity to minister within the body.

--Peter Pendall

Grief Recovery® is a ministry that helps individuals as well as helps individuals help others walk through the journey of Grief Recovery®.

--Mark Jones

And the value to our team is that if it works with us, it is going to circulate down to the lay people, and that I am excited about.

--Al Riley

I am delighted with the Grief Recovery® program and Nancy Stutz-Martin and all that they do to help believers, as well as those not yet trusting Christ, to understand their own hearts and to deal with the issues that are there.

--Peter Pendall

I am here because I believe in the Grief Recovery® process. I believe there is a lot of healing that needs to take place that God wants to bring to the hearts of men and women.

--Glenn Murphy

I am seeing people set free from bondage and hurts that they may not have known they've had their entire lives, but [now they are] finally able to face those things and be able to walk through them.

--Mark Jones

By the end of the process we learned how to speak the emotional truth from our hearts to one another, and it was a turning point in our staff relationship. I think we all look back at that time and say it was a turning point where we suddenly, and for the first time, began to function as a team instead of as collection of individuals.

--Glenn Murphy

Grief Recovery® is good for everybody, from the person who knows they have it all together, to the person who knows they have nothing left, to everybody in between. All can be helped and encouraged by this ministry.

--Mark Jones

I have to say it has been a real life saver for us as a staff.

--Peter Pendall

Grief Recovery® helps people end up on the

road of being set free from things that hold them down, things that are stopping them from being able to blossom to be the people that God created them to be.

--Mark Jones

CHAPTER 20
SEMINARY WORK

My ultimate goal when God gave me the vision of healing the body of Christ was to have Grief Recovery® skills taught in seminaries. I believe that the future of the church depends on it. We need to open up our hearts and learn to be transparent, so that the next generation will see a better example of people living as Christ taught us to live.

What I see happening in the seminaries in America today is that men and women are being given enormous amounts of intellectual knowledge about God and His Word, but few seem to be able to transfer that head knowledge to their hearts. Sadly, too many don't know how to relate to people.

I designed a course to be taught at the seminary level called: "Transformational Skills: Counseling through Grief, Loss, and Change."

In the fall of 2006, I taught the course at

Covington Seminary in Fort Oglethorpe, Georgia. I had five students in the class. It was amazing the level of trust that was established during the first class. The experience overwhelmingly proved the need for these skills among seminary students and the difference in their ability to connect their heads and their hearts and relate to other people in a more effective way, especially with those who are hurting.

During the last night of the class, I had a hard time getting the students to leave. One student commented, "This is the class you never want to end." I knew right then that I'd accomplished the goal God had given me: to change their lives forever for the Kingdom.

Here are the collective comments and evaluations from the seminary students. They were anonymous, so that students would be encouraged to be truthful.

* * * *

Grieving, in my opinion, was something to be handled on a private, individual basis. . . . a part of life that was between the griever and their Maker; a person just deals with grieving the best way they know how, tough it out, and eventually, get through it.

Engaging in helping grievers is a process that I feel is ordained by our Creator because He realizes the life-affecting consequences this has on us as individuals, as a local church body, and as a society. (II Corinthians 1:3-7 and Galatians 6:2).

* * * *

Since being in this class and working through the weekly exercises, my blood pressure readings have actually dropped and stayed down in the normal range on a consistent basis. The feelings of being uptight, stressed out, and, just generally wound up, have decreased in such a way that it has been noticed and commented on by my wife.

Unfortunately, most local churches today deal with a person's past by simply quoting 2 Corinthians 5:17 which says, "Old things are passed away." This verse is the inspired, infallible, inerrant word of God, but the behavior patterns, the defense mechanisms, the suppressed feelings, the losses and hurts of a person's life must be addressed.

I told you before, but I want to tell you again, this class has been a "Difference-Maker" in my life. I will recommend it to everyone who will listen to me.

* * * *

This class has radically changed my life, and as a result, I know I am a more effective follower of our Lord, a better man, a better husband and a better dad.

I can honestly say that the Lord used this class to radically change my heart and my understanding, relating to the grieving process, its profound impact on human lives, and the detrimental consequences of bad grieving versus healthy grieving.

I have learned that forgiveness is intended to take away the pain, but not the memory. I have learned that letting go is not the same as giving up. But I think above all else, the single most important lesson I have learned (using the death of my brother as a case study) is that Grief Recovery®, with proper teaching and guidance WORKS. This process has changed my life forever. It's through this process that I have made the incredible discovery that grief is processed through the heart, not the head, and when grieving is handled with this understanding as a central point, the result produces emotional healing.

* * * *

I was a griever and didn't know I was or that I needed help before taking this class. [Now] I am more at peace with myself. There is a kind of weight that has been lifted. I am not consumed by the weight all the time.

My wife says I seem more at peace; not letting what my ex-wife does have an effect on me like I used to. I do not get in a state of depression because of her actions. I am happier and more content with my life, and I am more focused on achieving my goals.

Today I am not just free, but free indeed. I have been bound by unforgiveness for six years. I knew about unconditional love, but not unconditional forgiveness. I understood the verses that are true, but lacked the wisdom to know how to apply the knowledge of the truth. I felt like the Ethiopian eunuch: "How can I know except some man show me?" I needed a practical application to apply the truth of God's Word in my life where I needed it.

Until I can overcome the past, I am bound.

Sometimes God allows hardships and circumstances in our lives that will press our hearts to reveal their hidden contents. Through God's illumination, the broken areas in our hearts can be cleansed, forgiven, healed, and strengthened. It is not for our benefit alone, but for blessings for our families and communities. Hurting people produce a hurting church, which affects homes, families, business relationships, etc. We need healthy Christians to have a healthy church.

* * * *

Before this class, I would always compare losses of individuals. I thought that losses were not equal, and people needed to see that there is always someone who has it worse. I guess in some ways I thought that this technique should help people, even myself. I have learned that people's individual grief shapes and molds their personalities.

People need to realize that holding grief inside has cheated them from being who God wants them to be. Without emotional healing you can never truly teach the lessons of forgiveness, and to me, that is one of the cornerstones of the Body of Christ. Without forgiveness, you can never really experience true love.

The greatest information that I have learned in this class is the freedom of forgiveness.

* * * *

My view of helping grievers has changed completely. I used to believe all of the old sayings that you would hear one person tell another person who was grieving. Such as, "Give it time;" "Just get over it;" "He or she is in a better place;" "There will be someone else;" etc.; I had never heard of it as "undelivered emotional communication."

Getting saved does not automatically fix things or the past. But churches and their staff sometimes seem to believe it does.

If would have been nice to have learned all of this information about Grief Recovery® a long time ago.

"We were created in His image as processing plants not storage tanks." Statements like that and others stick in my mind, like, "We all experience pain at 100%, so do not compare losses."

* * * *

In my personal opinion, grief or loss is the root problem for all the problems people face today, whether it concerns issues of addiction, divorce, death, or stress.

As a result of this class my outlook on life has changed tremendously. As we went through each step, I began to realize that I not only needed this class to help others, I needed this class for myself. It was amazing how much excess baggage, and how many unresolved issues I had so neatly hidden inside. My emotional pot was overflowing.

I am learning how to listen, not only with my head, but with my heart.

My wife has said that she can see a big difference in my attitude because I don't seem as stressed. I feel like my personality has changed. I have always been insecure about what people think about me. I think the reason for this was I didn't like myself. Now, I don't worry about this as much, because I have a better opinion of myself. I also wanted others to acknowledge my accomplishments, so I would feel good. The only one I want to please now is God.

I cannot get over the difference in the way I feel. My blood pressure does not fluctuate as it did before.

It feels so good to know that I am able to process the problems of everyday life in a much more positive way. The best part is that I am a much more emotionally stable person.

My pastor can tell I really love what I'm doing and can see the passion I have for helping those who are in need and looking for someone to be a listener and a mediator for God.

I really feel that God's way to deal with grief and pain from everyday life is the only way. He knows our pain already. All we need to do is express it to Him, lay it at His feet, and in magnificent grace, He will answer our prayers. One of the ways I began to realize this was because of one of our first journal questions. "If I don't know myself, how can I know God?"

We, as counselors, are just His servants who have been equipped to help our brothers and sisters with their needs.

I will never forget how the pain and grief I was harboring inside was hurting me and holding me back physically, emotionally, mentally, and most of all, spiritually. I feel like I've been let out of prison.

.

CHAPTER 21
GLOBAL HEALING: ISRAEL

In August of 2001, I began thinking about how life-giving it would be to have a Jewish, Arab, and Christian Grief Recovery® Trainer working in Israel. I was ready to be the Christian Grief Recovery® Trainer, and I also knew a Jewish Grief Recovery® Trainer who was available, but I didn't know of an Arab Grief Recovery® Trainer. So I, and some prayer partners, began asking God to send us an Arab to be trained.

Three weeks later at the American Association of Christian Counselors (AACC) meeting in Nashville, Tennessee, I met Chrissie Sheehan. Chrissie is from Dalton, Georgia and is a missionary to Israel. Her mother is a Southern Belle, and her father is of Arabic descent. Chrissie usually spends nine months in Israel and returns to the States for the summer. She was as excited as I was, and happily went through the Grief Recovery® Certification Class. She also began helping me with other classes, so that she could sharpen her skills before returning to Israel.

At that time Israel had minimal resources to help the believers deal with the emotional issues of daily life. So she began bringing Messianic Jews (Jews who believe in Christ as the Messiah, also called "completed Jews"), who needed healing to the Chattanooga, Tennessee area, so that I and others could work with them.

The results of this Grief Recovery® work made such an impact in the lives of these people that the pastors of their churches requested that I bring the Grief Recovery® program to Israel. So at the invitation of various congregations in Israel, I began my ministry to the Holy Land.

Tony Sperandeo is the pastor of a congregation in Far Saba. The congregation is a mix of Jewish, Russian, and other ethnic groups. He'd asked me to speak during the service and explain to his people what I'd come there to do. As I stood before them, sharing the message of hope and healing that God had given me, they began to weep. It was overwhelming to see how they responded when they learned why it was so important not to bury the past and how it affects our intimacy with Yeshua (Hebrew for Jesus). After the service, thirty congregants signed up for the Grief Recovery® Workshop.

Workshops are usually limited to fourteen people. I explained to Pastor Tony that with thirty people in the class, it would be very difficult to provide safety and personal ministry to everyone. So he and I worked out a compromise, and twenty people attended the Grief Recovery® Workshop. Chrissie assisted me, and with the use of interpreters, the workshop was translated into five languages: Hebrew, Russian, Portuguese, French, and Finnish. Pastor Tony and his wife, Orna, also attended. Tony felt strongly that he, as the church leader, should be willing to set the example for his congregation. And, of course, I agreed with him!

Several personal responses from the participants of the Grief Recovery® Workshop are included below. I've chosen *not* to edit their English, so the purity of their hearts would shine through.

No words. You've captured areas of my heart I thought were beyond reaching feeling and have drawn them close to the Lord. Thank you for teaching me how to begin. Thank you for opening the doors of life through acknowledgment of death. I love you sincerely, and thank you for pouring forth your time, energy, emotion, prayer, wisdom and heart for this time. This is emotional truth. --A.S.

Thank you for bringing light and fragrance in the dark and painful place in my heart. Also for giving me the tools in my toolbox (pearl in my treasure chest). I Love You, --J.H.

God bless you for doing what you do! It helped me a lot! You are truly doing the service of the Lord. I pray you will return.--E.R.

You are a gift to the Body and to Israel. The country needs the wonderful grace and unconditional love that you have.--D.S.

If my dad was attending your seminar...the world would be much better. Thank you.--T.L.

I see you as one that is planted at the tree near the water, to refresh burdened souls in His strength. Thank you for sharing your refreshing life with me. We thank the Lord for you. --R.D.

Thank you for being the tool to bring us to more freedom from our past. We love you and bless you in the name of the Lord.--Pastor Tony & Orna

The second Grief Recovery® Workshop was held in Modiin. Fifteen people attended. Wanting to set an example for their Modiin congregation, Pastor Fred and Eva attended. One of the participants in the class was a social worker who worked with children at a local hospital. Her story poignantly shows the effectiveness of the Grief Recovery® process when believers tap into the power of the Holy Spirit.

Sarah's father had died when she was twelve years old. In the typical Jewish tradition known as sitting *Shiva*, the family mourned for seven days. During this time, mirrors are covered with blankets, and grievers take cushions off of couches, so they can sit lower to the ground. Women don't wear make-up or do their hair. Everyone is meant to mourn wholeheartedly and with abandon. At the end of the seven days, Sarah was told she was not to cry anymore.

She still missed her father terribly, so when no one was around, she would climb into the closet and wrap herself in his shirts that still hung in the closet. She could smell her father's fragrance among his clothes. But eventually, her mother removed his clothes from the house. Sarah stuffed all the pain and memories deep down inside, so that she could go on.

At the end of the Grief Recovery® Workshop, as the group was debriefing (having the opportunity to process the experience), Sarah remarked, "After reading my completion letter to my dad, I closed my eyes to get a clear picture of him and say goodbye as you had instructed us to do. Incredible! As I did, I could smell my dad again!"

The need for Grief Recovery® in Israel, as you can well imagine, is overwhelming. One person traveling back and forth to Israel to offer the Grief Recovery® Workshops was never going to reach the masses. It was apparent to all that we needed to provide an opportunity for individuals living in Israel to become certified as Grief Recovery® Specialists. This would allow them to offer *ongoing* services.

I returned home and shared my experiences with John James and Russell Friedman, my associates at The Grief Recovery Institute. I offered to provide all my services at no cost to The Grief Recovery Institute if they would allow me to return and train people living there. They agreed, and helped to raise the money to have five thousand copies of *The Grief Recovery Handbook* translated into Hebrew as a *gift* to the nation! The following year, I returned to Israel and began training Internationals and Jews in the skills of Grief Recovery®.

Many participants were from several Messianic Congregations and ministries, and some work specifically with terrorist victims and their families.

All are key people to provide Grief Recovery® classes to a variety of different populations.

.

NOTES

[1] Eph. 3:16-19 (NIV).

[2] John W. James and Russell Friedman, The Grief Recovery® Outreach Manual, 2002.

[3] John W. James and Russell Friedman, The Grief Recovery Handbook (New York: HarperCollins, 1998) 5.

[4] James, 5.

[5] Jessica Shaver, "I Told God I Was Angry," Resilience, ed. H. Norman Wright (Ann Arbor: Servant Publications, 1997) 58.

[6] Nancy Stutz-Martin, "Prophetic Word for the Bishops," The Joint College of African-American Pentecostal Bishops, Bertram Conference Center, Aurora, Ohio, March 16-17, 2005.

[7] Dwight L. Carlson, Why Do Christians Shoot Their

Wounded? (Downers Grove: Intervarsity, 1994) 56.

[8] T.D. Jakes, Naked and Not Ashamed (Shippensburg: Destiny Image, 1995) 135.

[9] "Guilt," Merriam Webster's Collegiate Dictionary, 1993 ed.

[10] James, 3.

[11] James, 3.

[12] Dan Allender and Tremper Longman III, Cry of the Soul (Dallas: Word P, 1994) 24-25.

[13] John W. James, Russell Friedman, with Dr. Leslie Landon Matthews, When Children Grieve (New York: HarperCollins, 2001) 16-17.

[14] Prov. 4:23 (NASB-U).

[15] Luke 8:15 (NASB-U).

[16] Ezek. 36:26 (NASB-U).

[17] William P. Cheshire, Jr., M.D., "He Knoweth the Secrets of the Heart," Restore (Summer 1996) 12-14.

[18] 1 Cor. 1:22-24 (NASB).

[19] 1 Cor. 2: 1-4 (NASB).

[20] Colin Brown, <u>The New International Dictionary of New Testament Theology</u>, Vol. II (Grand Rapids: Zondervan, 1996) 80.

[21] Matt. 22:37 (NASB).

[22] Luke 21:34 (NASB).

[23] Jer. 17:10 (NASB).

[24] Heb. 4:12-13 (NASB).
[25] Jer. 29:13 (NASB).

[26] Peter Scazzero, <u>Emotionally Healthy Spirituality</u> (Franklin:Integrity, 2006) 12.

[27] Ps. 51:10 (NASB-U).

[28] Ps. 95:8 (NASB-U).

[29] Ex. 17:1-7 (NASB).

[30] Mark 6:52 (NASB-U).

[31] Mark 10:2-5 (NASB-U).

[32] Mark 16:14 (NASB-U).

[33] Rom. 2:4-5 (NASB-U).

[34] Heb. 12:15-17 (NASB-U).

[35] Deut. 10:16 (NASB-U).

[36] Jer. 4:4 (NASB-U).

[37] Ps. 139:23-24 (NASB-U).

[38] Gen. 6:6 (NASB-U).

[39] Gen. 3:21 (NASB-U).

[40] Isa. 53:3 (NASB-U).

[41] Mark 14:36 (NASB-U).

[42] Matt. 27:46 (NASB-U).

[43] Eph. 4:30 (NASB-U).

[44] Eccles. 3:4 (NASB).

[45] 2 Thess. 4:13 (NASB).

[46] James, The Grief Recovery Handbook, 35.

[47] James, 35.

[48] James, 77-78.

[49] James, 78.

[50] James, 82.

[51] Peter Scazzero, Emotionally Healthy Spirituality, 24-25.

[52] James, 79.

[53] Isa. 1:5 (NLT).

[54] James, 80.

[55] James, 80.

[56] James, 6-7.

[57] Phil. 3:13 (NASB-U).

[58] Steve Chapman, "The Secret Place," prod. Don Potter, Family Favorites (SACD-105, Careers-BMG Music P, Shepherds Fold Music BMI, 1981).

[59] James, 115.

[60] James, 116.

[61] James, 116.

[62] Psm. 51:6 (NASB-U).

[63] James, 110.

[64] James, 110.

[65] James, 110-111.

[66] James, 111.

[67] Col. 1:28 (NASB-U).

[68] James, 116-117.

[69] James, 96.

[70] Lewis Smedes, How Can It Be All Right When

Everything's All Wrong? (San Francisco: Harper San Francisco, 1992) 43.

[71] "Forgive" and "Condone," Merriam Webster's Collegiate Dictionary, 1993 ed.

[72] Luke 12:34 (NASB-U).

[73] 2 Cor. 2:10-11 (NASB-U).

[74] Peter Scazzero, Emotionally Healthy Church (Grand Rapids: Zondervan, 2003) 130.

[75] Rom. 12:18 (NASB).

[76] Ps. 51:1-6 (NIV).

[77] Peter Scazzero, Emotionally Healthy Church, 10-11.

[78] Jas. 5:16 (NASB-U).

[79] Mal. 2:5 (NIV).

[80] Mal. 2:6 (NIV).

[81] Nancy Stutz-Martin, Personal Journal (2/15/07).

[82] Sarah Young, Jesus Calling (Brentwood: Integrity, 2004) 96.

[83] Peter Scazzero, Emotionally Healthy Church, 29.

[84] Larry Crabb, Shattered Dreams (Colorado

Springs: Waterhouse, 2001) 209.

[85] Psm. 46:1 (NASB-U).

[86] Alan Jamieson, <u>A Churchless Faith: Faith Journeys Beyond the Churches</u> (Great Britain: Society for Promoting Christian Knowledge,_2002) 16.

[87] Ron Sider, <u>The Scandal of the Evangelical Conscience: Why Are Christians Living Just like the Rest of the World?</u> (Grand Rapids:_Baker Books, 2005) 13.

[88] Sider, 29-29.

[89] Scazzero, <u>Emotionally Healthy Church</u>, 78.

[90] John Eldredge, <u>The Journey of Desire</u> (Nashville: Thomas Nelson, 2000) 189.

[91] Psm. 126-4-6 (NLT).

[92] Isa. 45:3 (NIV).

.

BIBLIOGRAPHY

Allender, Dan and Tremper Longman III. <u>Cry of the Soul</u>. Dallas: Word, 1994.

Brown, Colin. <u>The New International Dictionary of New Testament Theology</u>. Vol. 2. Grand Rapids: Zondervan, 1986.

Carlson, Dwight L. <u>Why Do Christians Shoot Their Wounded?</u> Downers Grove: Intervarsity, 1994.

Chapman, Steve. "The Secret Place." Prod. Don Potter. <u>Family Favorites</u>. SACD-105. Careers-BMG Music Publishing, Shepherds Fold Music/BMI, 1981.

Cheshire, William P. Jr., M.D. "He Knoweth the Secrets of the Heart." <u>Restore</u>. Summer 1996.

"Condone," "Forget," "Guilt." <u>Merriam Webster's Collegiate Dictionary</u>. 1993 ed.

Crabb, Larry. <u>Shattered Dreams</u>. Colorado Springs: Waterhouse, 2001.

Eldredge, John. <u>The Journey of Desire</u>. Nashville: Thomas Nelson, 2000.

James, T.D. <u>Naked and Not Ashamed</u>. Shippensburg: Destiny Image, 1995.

James, John W. and Russell Friedman. <u>The Grief Recovery Handbook</u>. New York: HarperCollins,

1988.

James, John W. and Russell Friedman with Dr. Leslie Landon Matthews. When Children Grieve. New York: HarperCollins, 2001.

James, John W. and Russell Friedman. The Grief Recovery ® Outreach Program Manual, 2002.

Jamieson, Alan. A Churchless Faith: Faith Journeys Beyond the Churches. Great Britain: Society for Promoting Christian Knowledge, 2002.

Scazzero, Peter. Emotionally Healthy Spirituality. Franklin: Integrity, 2006.

Scazzero, Peter. The Emotionally Healthy Church. Grand Rapids: Zondervan, 2003.

Shaver, Jessica. "I Told God I Was Angry." Resilience. Ed. H. Norman Wright. Ann Arbor: Servant Publications, 1997.

Smedes, Lewis. How Can It Be All Right When Everything's All Wrong? San Francisco: Harper San Francisco, 1992.

Sider, Ron. The Scandal of the Evangelical Conscience: Why Are Christians Living Just Like the Rest of the World? Grand Rapids: Baker Books, 2005.

Stutz-Martin, Nancy. "Prophetic Word for the Bishops." The Joint College of African-American Pentecostal Bishops. Bertram Conference Center,

Aurora, Ohio. March 14-15, 2005.

Young, Sarah. <u>Jesus Calling</u>. Brentwood: Integrity, 2004.

ABOUT THE AUTHOR,
NANCY STUTZ-MARTIN

Nancy went to be with her Lord and Savior on May 29, 2018.

She was many things to many people. She was a wife to Tony and the mother of John. She was active in the faith community. She was the founder of Sunrise at Midnight, an organization that provided educational resources for clergy and members of the faith community around the world, many of which were based on the teachings of The Grief Recovery Method. She was a Certified Grief Recovery Specialist and a Grief Recovery Certification Trainer. She was a friend and mentor to everyone she met!

Nancy had a strong educational background, as is outlined on the **Sunrise at Midnight** website. "Nancy received her Doctoral Degree in Christian Counseling from Covington Theological Seminary, a Master's Degree from Vanderbilt University and did post graduate training at Sloan Kettering Cancer Institute, The Grief Recovery Institute, and Harvard Medical School. She was an educator, researcher and author. Nancy [was] a board certified Psychiatric Nurse Practitioner, maintained a private practice, and consulted extensively for hospice, the medical community, schools, and the faith-based community. She [was] a professor at Covington Seminary, and a member of the American Association of Christian Counselors. These are her "facts," but hardly tell the story of how she touched people, not only in The United States, but worldwide with her message for a better tomorrow.

I had the pleasure of meeting Nancy in the early 2000's at the old Grief Recovery Institute offices in Sherman Oaks, California. She and I had both been "on the road" with John James, as two of the first three people from outside the Institute who had been invited to become Certification Trainers. We were both attending a Certification Training with Russell Friedman, as we continued to prepare for this new adventure in our lives. I remember well her excitement in learning how to share this new-found knowledge with others.

As Nancy traveled the world, in her mission work with her church, she never missed an opportunity to share the message of The Grief Recovery Method with others. She fully recognized that this unique approach to dealing with the pain of emotional loss was not a "faith based" approach, but one that could still be used by people of every faith.

In Israel, she worked with the Messianic Congregation leadership to provide Certification Training. She expanded this to offer reconciliation work among the Arab and Jewish communities.

John James remembers that she even distributed Arabic translations of the Grief Recovery Handbook to refugees, in an effort to help them deal with the emotional pain of the losses they had experienced.

It was in **Africa that she made her greatest international impact.** While on a mission trip, she met with pastors and saw, first hand, the grief related impact that poverty, starvation, disease, AIDS and war had on the people of that continent. She developed a vision of how the Grief Recovery Method could make a real difference and approached John, Russell and Cole about doing trainings in Africa. Despite all of the logistical obstacles she encountered, she made it work! Africa now has a network of specialists providing that badly needed emotional support, thanks to the work of Nancy Stutz-Martin.

She may have physically left us, but she still plays a vital role in supporting Grief Recovery Specialists. You can still watch her videos about bringing the Grief Recovery Method into church settings under the "GRM Continued Learning" tab on the section of the Grief Recovery Method website reserved for Certified Personnel.

Nancy stated on her personal business website that she never found a wall in her path that she could not find a way over, around or through! Her faith and personal conviction to the power of the Grief Recovery message never allowed her to falter in her quest to help others. Even when her health caused her to step away from being a Certification Trainer, she continued to support others, in the United States and around the world in taking Recovery Action.

Nancy will be greatly missed by all who were touched by her work, but her legacy will live on for generations to come!

You can read more about Nancy's work bringing the Grief Recovery Method to Africa or by visiting her website, Sunrise at Midnight-The Africa Project.

Note: This eulogy was written by Mr. Stephen Moeller, of The Grief Recovery Method and has given us permission to reprint it in this book. Please see their website for more information about The Grief Recovery Method. https://www.griefrecoverymethod.com

For those in the Chattanooga area who are

interested in learning more about The Grief Recovery Method, visit http://www.griefchatt.com. The White Oak United Methodist Church, 2232 Lyndon Avenue, Chattanooga, TN hosts the Chattanooga Center for Grief Recovery. 423-779-6420. You may also email for additional information at: info@GriefChatt.com.

Made in the USA
Lexington, KY
15 December 2019